# AI and Theological Pedagogy

# AI and Theological Pedagogy

## A Bloom's Taxonomy Approach for Graduate Seminaries

under the supervision of
**Heather Shellabarger**

*Theological Essentials*

©Digital Theological Library 2025
Library of Congress Cataloging-in-Publication Data


Heather Shellabarger (creator).
AI and Theological Pedagogy: A Bloom's Taxonomy Approach for
Graduate Seminaries / Heather Shellabarger

138 + x pp. cm. 12.7 x 20.32
ISBN 979-8-89731-147-7 (Print)
ISBN 979-8-89731-176-7 (Ebook)
ISBN 979-8-89731-170-5 (Kindle)
ISBN 979-8-89731-157-6 (Abridged Audio Discussion)
1.  Theological seminaries—Study and teaching (Graduate)
2.  Theology—Study and teaching (Graduate)
3.  Artificial intelligence—Educational applications
BV 4012 .S54 2025

*This book is available in other languages at*
*www.DTLPress.com*

Cover Image: "The Forthcoming Seminary Classroom" Image produced by
the author using AI

# Contents

# Series Preface

Artificial Intelligence (AI) is changing everything, including theological scholarship and education. This series, *Theological Essentials*, is designed to bring the creative potential of AI to the field of theological education. In the traditional model, a scholar with both mastery of the scholarly discourse and a record of successful classroom teaching would spend several months—or even several years—writing, revising and rewriting an introductory text which would then be transferred to a publisher who also invested months or years in production processes. Even though the end product was typically quite predictable, this slow and expensive process caused the prices of textbooks to balloon. As a result, students in developed nations paid more than they should have for the books and students in developing nations typically had no access to these (cost-prohibitive) textbooks until they appeared as discards and donations decades later. In previous generations, the need for quality assurance—in the form of content generation, expert review, copy-editing and printing time—may have made this slow, expensive and exclusionary approach inevitable. However, AI is changing everything.

This series is very different; it is created by AI. The cover of each volume identifies the work as "created under the supervision of" an expert in the field. However, that person is not an author in the traditional sense. The creator of each volume has been trained by the DTL staff in the use of AI and *the creator has used AI to create, edit, revise and recreate the text that you see*. With that creation process clearly identified, let me explain the goals of this series.

## Our Goals:

*Credibility:* Although AI has made—and continues to make—huge strides over the last few years, no unsupervised AI can create a truly reliable or fully credible college or seminary level text. The limitations of AI generated content sometimes originates from the limitations of the content itself (the training set may be inadequate), but more often, user dissatisfaction with AI-generated content arises from human errors associated with poor prompt engineering. The DTL Press has sought to overcome both of these problems by hiring established scholars with widely recognized expertise to create books within their areas of expertise and by training those scholars and experts in AI prompt engineering. To be clear, the scholar whose name appears on the cover of this work has created this volume—generating, reading, regenerating, rereading and revising the work. Even though the work was generated (in varying degrees) by AI, the names of our scholarly creators appear on the cover as a guarantee that the content is equally credible with any introductory work which that scholar/creator would pen using the traditional model.

*Stability:* AI is generative, meaning that the response to each prompt is uniquely generated for that specific request. No two AI-generated responses are precisely the same. The inevitable variability of AI responses presents a significant pedagogical challenge for professors and students who wish to begin their discussions and analysis on the basis of a shared set of ideas. Educational institutions need stable texts in order to prevent pedagogical chaos. These books provide that stable text from which to teach, discuss and engage ideas.

*Affordability:* The DTL Press is committed to the idea that affordability should not be a barrier to knowledge. *All persons are equally deserving of the right to know and to understand.* Therefore, ebook versions of all DTL Press books are available from the DTL libraries without charge, and available as print books for a nominal fee. Our scholar/creators are to be thanked for their willingness to forego traditional royalty arrangements. (Our creators are compensated for their generative work, but they do not receive royalties in the traditional sense.)

*Accessibility:* The DTL Press would like to make high quality, low cost introductory textbooks available to everyone, everywhere in the world. The books in this series are immediately made available in multiple languages. The DTL Press will create translations in other languages upon request. Translations are, of course, generated by AI.

### *Our Acknowledged Limitations:*

Some readers are undoubtedly thinking, "but AI can only produce derivative scholarship; AI can't create original, innovative scholarship." That criticism is, of course, largely accurate. AI is largely limited to aggregating, organizing and repackaging pre-existing ideas (although sometimes in ways that can be used to accelerate and refine the production of original scholarship). Still while acknowledging this inherent limitation of AI, the DTL Press would offer two comments: (1) Introductory texts are seldom meant to be truly ground breaking in their originality and (2) the DTL Press has other series dedicated to publishing original scholarship with traditional authorship.

## Our Invitation:

The DTL Press would like to fundamentally reshape academic publishing in the theological world to make scholarship more accessible and more affordable in two ways. First, we would like to generate introductory texts in all areas of theological discourse, so that no one is ever forced to "buy a textbook" in any language. It is our vision for professors anywhere to be able to use one book, two books or an entire set of books in this series as the *introductory* textbooks for their classes. Second, we would also like to publish traditionally authored scholarly monographs for Open Access (free) distribution for an advanced scholarly readership.

Finally, the DTL Press is non-confessional and will publish works in any area of religious studies. Traditionally authored books are peer-reviewed; AI-generated introductory book creation is open to anyone with the required expertise to supervise content generation in that area of discourse. If you share the DTL Press's commitment to credibility, affordability and accessibility, contact us about changing the world of theological publishing by contributing to this series or a more traditionally authored series.

With high expectations,

*Thomas E. Phillips*

DTL Press Executive Director
www.thedtl.org
www.DTLpress.com

# Introduction
## Teaching at the Crossroads of Theology and Technology

Theological education has always been shaped by the tools and contexts of its time. From the oral traditions of the early Church to the scriptoria of medieval monasteries, from the printing press that launched the Reformation to the rise of online education in the 21st century, each era has confronted the question: How do we faithfully form ministers, scholars, and leaders for the Church amid cultural and technological change?

We are now living through one of the most significant shifts in the history of human learning, the rise of artificial intelligence. Language models can now generate sermons. Algorithms can compose prayers. AI tutors can explain Scripture, translate Hebrew, simulate pastoral care conversations, and draft theological outlines in seconds. These tools, once unthinkable, are increasingly woven into the daily lives of students, educators, and pastors alike. The classroom is no longer bound by four walls or a fixed schedule. Knowledge is no longer scarce, and the role of the teacher is no longer simply to transmit information.

In this moment, theological educators are being called to a new kind of wisdom: a pedagogy that is both ancient and adaptive, one that draws on the richness of tradition while engaging emerging tools with critical discernment. This book seeks to offer such a framework. It is a guide for graduate-level theological educators — seminary professors, curriculum designers, and institutional leaders—who want to teach faithfully and effectively in the age of artificial intelligence.

Our approach is grounded in Bloom's Taxonomy, a time-tested framework for structuring learning objectives and assessing cognitive development. Yet this taxonomy is more than an instructional strategy—it is a spiritual and pedagogical invitation to walk with students from surface learning to deep integration, from remembering texts to embodying wisdom. Each chapter explores one of Bloom's domains—remembering, understanding, applying, analyzing, evaluating, and creating—and shows how AI can be integrated to support learning while forming students for theological reflection and faithful ministry.

But this book does not stop with Bloom. It also explores the broader theological, spiritual, and communal questions that arise when artificial intelligence enters the classroom. Can AI shape souls? What does authorship mean in an age of generative tools? How do we safeguard formation, attention, and discernment in a culture of speed and automation? What guidelines should govern responsible AI use in seminary education?

We contend that theological education is not merely about mastering content. It is about cultivating character, forming spiritual depth, and preparing students to lead communities with humility, courage, and hope. Technology must serve these goals, not undermine them. When guided by a robust theological vision, AI can become a tool for liberation, accessibility, and creativity. But if left unexamined, it can also erode community, hollow out vocation, and dull theological imagination.

This book is written in the spirit of invitation and exploration. It is not a manual of best practices, nor a defense of digital utopianism. Rather, it is a theological provocation: What might it mean to teach theologically in the age of AI? What kind of faculty, students, and institutions will emerge when we blend ancient formation with new technologies? What must we hold fast to, and what must we be willing to reimagine?

The task before us is not simply to update our syllabi. It is to reexamine our calling as educators considering emerging tools, shifting epistemologies, and the enduring work of spiritual formation. As we step into this new era, may we do so with courage, clarity, and deep trust in the One who remains the true Teacher of us all.

# Chapter 1
# A Theological Vision for Teaching and Learning

## Introduction: Teaching as Sacred Vocation

Teaching in a theological context is not merely the act of delivering content — it is a sacred participation in God's work of formation. Christian educators do not simply transmit facts; they cultivate wisdom, nurture vocation, and foster the discernment necessary for faithful service in the Church and the world. In this light, the seminary classroom becomes a site of discipleship, where students are invited into a deeper journey of knowing God, loving others, and bearing witness to the gospel.

In our time, this vocation is undergoing transformation. Artificial intelligence, digital learning platforms, and global shifts in educational delivery present both profound opportunities and deep questions. How do we maintain our commitment to Spirit-led formation while engaging with new technologies? How do we ensure that teaching remains relational, contextual, and spiritually formative?

This chapter lays the theological foundation for these questions, focusing on three themes: the enduring purpose of theological education in a digital age; the biblical and theological vision that shapes our understanding of formation and instruction; and the calling of the educator to teach with wisdom, humility, and innovation.

### The Purpose of Theological Education in a Digital Age

Theological education has always served a dual purpose: the formation of faithful ministers and the nurturing of theological wisdom for the sake of the Church's witness. These purposes remain unchanged, but the context in which they are pursued has shifted dramatically. We live in an age of information saturation, moral fragmentation, and rapid technological innovation. Digital tools — from smartphones to artificial intelligence — are reshaping how people relate to truth, authority, community, and even themselves.

In this environment, the purpose of theological education must be both resilient and reimagined. It must be resilient in its commitment to the historic task of preparing people for gospel ministry: forming students who can rightly handle the Word of truth, shepherd God's people with wisdom and compassion, and bear faithful witness in a broken world. But it must also be reimagined considering the realities of a digital culture that prizes speed over depth, novelty over faithfulness, and connectivity over community.

Today's seminary students are not simply learning for ministry, they are being spiritually and psychologically shaped by the digital tools they use every day. These tools influence how they think, how they relate, and how they imagine the world. As a result, theological education must not only inform their minds; it must form their imaginations, cultivating habits of attentiveness, critical discernment, and theological reflection that resist the shallow logic of the algorithm.

In this context, theological education must aim to foster deep theological literacy in a time when many rely on surface-level, search-engine knowledge. It must also cultivate spiritual formation amid the constant noise and distraction of digital life, helping students recover habits of prayer, reflection, and presence. Furthermore, it must develop pastoral imagination in an era where human relationships are increasingly mediated through screens, guiding future ministers in learning how to care, counsel, and lead with empathy and theological depth. Finally, it must form resilient and reflective leaders who can minister with wisdom and courage amid cultural fragmentation, ecclesial transition, and moral ambiguity.

The digital age also presents opportunities: tools that can support learning, expand access, and simulate real-world ministry experiences. Artificial intelligence, when used thoughtfully, can assist students in mastering languages, testing ideas, visualizing historical and theological connections, and receiving feedback on their work. But these tools must remain in service to the larger goal: formation into Christlikeness and preparation for wise leadership.

Theological education, then, is not simply about the transfer of content. It is about cultivating Christ-centered wisdom in the digital wilderness. It is about shaping ministers who can speak the truth in love — whether from a pulpit, in a hospital room, on a Zoom call, or in a digitally-mediated conversation — and who are grounded enough in the gospel to lead others with courage, humility, and clarity.

The Seminary must be more than a graduate school; it must be a formational community where students are prepared not only to know the faith but to embody it in a world that is desperately seeking hope and meaning. In this light, the purpose of theological education is not merely academic — it is ecclesial, pastoral, and missional, called to serve the Church and the world in the name of Christ.

## Biblical and Theological Frameworks for Formation and Instruction

The work of teaching in a theological context must be grounded not only in pedagogical technique but in a rich biblical and theological vision of formation. Christian education is, at its core, a ministry of discipleship—a Spirit-empowered process by which individuals are shaped into the likeness of Christ and prepared to participate in God's redemptive mission in the world. This formation includes intellectual development, but it cannot be reduced to cognitive mastery. It is holistic, involving the renewal of the mind, the transformation of character, and the cultivation of a life aligned with the purposes of God.

Scripture offers numerous images of teaching that are both instructive and inspiring. Moses, standing before the people of Israel, teaches them to remember, obey, and pass on the covenantal wisdom of God. The Psalms repeatedly celebrate those who meditate on God's Law, day and night, whose lives are rooted like trees planted by streams of living water. Jesus, the master teacher, forms His disciples not through lectures alone but through stories, questions, meals, and shared life. His teaching integrates word and deed, doctrine and love, calling and formation. The Apostle Paul continues this model, exhorting the early churches with theological instruction grounded in pastoral concern, always with an eye toward building up the body of Christ into maturity.

The Church's theological tradition reinforces this integrative vision. Augustine believed that teaching was not only the communication of knowledge but the ordering of love—helping learners grow in their desire for God and neighbor. For him, effective teaching stirs the affections and orients the will toward the highest good. Later, thinkers such as Aquinas emphasized that

8

theology is not only a science but a spiritual discipline — a pursuit of understanding rooted in faith and nourished by prayer. In more contemporary settings, theological education has been recognized as a task that must serve the life of the Church and resist fragmentation between academic theology and lived faith.

This vision challenges educators to see their work as both intellectual and pastoral, academic and ecclesial. Every syllabus, lecture, and classroom encounter should reflect a commitment to forming persons, not just producing graduates. Formation happens not only through what is taught, but through how it is taught and who is doing the teaching. The integrity of the educator, the relational dynamics of the classroom, and the practices embedded in the learning environment all contribute to shaping students for a life of discipleship and ministry.

At its best, theological instruction becomes an invitation to transformation — a pilgrimage of learning in community, guided by the Spirit, rooted in the Word, and oriented toward service in the world. It is not a neutral enterprise but one that is always shaping desires, identities, and practices. In this way, theological education becomes a participation in the ongoing work of God: forming a people who know the story of redemption, live it faithfully, and are prepared to bear witness to it in every sphere of life.

## The Educator's Calling: Wisdom, Humility, and Innovation

To teach theology is to participate in a holy trust — the passing on of the faith once delivered to the saints in a way that speaks to today's world with clarity, courage, and compassion. Theological educators stand not only in classrooms, but within the long tradition of the Church's teachers: pastors, prophets, scholars, and guides who have helped the people of God navigate seasons of change, conflict, and calling. In this tradition, the educator is not a mere content expert or lecturer. They are a steward of sacred mysteries, a companion on the path of formation, and a cultivator of wisdom in others.

This vocation demands wisdom — not simply as accumulated knowledge or academic achievement, but as the spiritual discernment to know what to teach, when to challenge, and how to care. Wisdom enables the educator to bring together doctrine and life, to hold space for questions without fear, and to guide students toward theological maturity. In an age marked by uncertainty and overload, educators must discern what truly forms, what distracts, and what endures.

Humility is just as essential. It allows the educator to teach from a posture of service rather than control, to admit limits, and to invite the Spirit into the learning process. The humble teacher recognizes that they are also a learner — continually shaped by Scripture, tradition, students, and the demands of a changing world. Humility resists the temptation to dominate the classroom and instead fosters a space where dialogue, curiosity, and spiritual growth can flourish.

In this rapidly evolving age, innovation is not optional, it is part of faithful stewardship. But theological innovation is not about chasing trends or adopting tools for novelty's sake. Rather, it involves a creative attentiveness to what will best serve formation. This may mean reimagining pedagogical methods, incorporating digital tools such as artificial intelligence to assist and personalize instruction, or crafting new learning environments that respond to students' diverse needs and cultural realities. Innovation becomes faithful when it is rooted in theological vision, responsive to contemporary challenges, and animated by the Spirit's ongoing work in the Church and the world.

To be a theological educator today is to live at the intersection of enduring truths and emerging questions. It is to teach in the tension between the already and the not yet grounded in the gospel, attentive to the moment, and hopeful for what the Spirit is doing. In this sacred work, wisdom, humility, and innovation are not optional virtues — they are the shape of faithfulness.

## Conclusion: Laying the Foundation

This chapter provides the foundation upon which the rest of the book is built. Theological teaching is sacred work, rooted in Scripture and tradition, oriented toward transformation, and always seeking to serve the Church.

In the chapters ahead, we will explore how Bloom's Taxonomy can help structure theological instruction for depth and growth; how AI can be engaged in pedagogically and spiritually meaningful ways; and how theological educators can design courses that reflect both excellence and care.

But before any of that, we must remember: our first calling is not to strategy, but to faithfulness — to God, to our students, and to the Church we serve.

# Chapter 2
## Bloom's Taxonomy and Theological Formation

### Introduction: Why Bloom's Taxonomy Matters for Theological Education

In the work of theological education, it is not enough to simply cover content. Formation requires thoughtful progression — guiding students from basic knowledge to deep spiritual and intellectual integration. Bloom's Taxonomy, a widely used educational framework, offers a valuable model for this movement. It outlines six levels of cognitive engagement: remembering, understanding, applying, analyzing, evaluating, and creating. Each level builds on the previous, forming a path from knowledge acquisition to theological imagination.

This chapter explores each level of Bloom's Taxonomy considering theological learning. It considers how theological educators can design instruction that honors both cognitive development and spiritual formation, and how artificial intelligence might serve — rather than short-circuit — these aims.

### Remembering: The Foundation of Theological Knowledge

Theological formation begins with remembering. This foundational level of learning involves more than rote memorization; it is a sacred act of recalling the truths of the faith, the stories of God's people, and the vocabulary that gives shape to theological understanding. In both Scripture and tradition, remembering is central to the life of faith. Israel is repeatedly called to remember the covenant, the Exodus, and the faithfulness of God. Jesus institutes the Lord's Supper as a ritual of remembrance. The early Church memorized creeds and catechisms not as academic exercises but as practices of communal identity and fidelity.

In the seminary classroom, remembering takes form in the memorization of Scripture passages, theological terms, historical timelines, and the ordering of doctrines. It lays the groundwork for all higher-order learning, enabling students to engage more deeply in understanding, interpretation, and application. A student cannot critically reflect on a doctrine they do not first know by heart, nor can they analyze theological arguments if they have no internal grasp of the key ideas and sources. Thus, remembering is not simplistic; it is foundational. It enables theological reflection to take root in memory and imagination.

Artificial intelligence offers a range of tools that can support this level of formation. Intelligent flashcard systems can reinforce vocabulary in biblical languages and theological terminology. AI-generated timelines can help students visualize key developments in Church history and doctrinal evolution. Interactive quizzes and chat-based review sessions can provide personalized feedback and repetition that strengthens retention. When designed with spiritual formation in mind, even these basic tools can become instruments of devotion—supporting not only academic performance but the kind of remembrance that nourishes faith and prepares students to teach others also.

Ultimately, remembering in theological education is an act of anchoring students in the memory of the Church, the story of salvation, and the character of God. It is the first step on the path toward wisdom and pastoral competence. Far from being mechanical or outdated, it is the sacred discipline of calling to mind the truths that shape who we are and how we minister.

## Understanding: Interpreting and Articulating Meaning

Understanding builds upon remembering by inviting students to make sense of what they have learned. It moves the learner from simple recall to meaningful interpretation. In theological education, this involves explaining concepts in one's own words, grasping the significance of doctrines, and discerning the internal logic of the Christian faith. Understanding is where theology becomes intelligible — not just a list of terms or dates, but a coherent vision of God's work in the world and the Church's participation in that work. At this stage, students begin to comprehend the "why" behind the "what," exploring how biblical texts, theological arguments, and historical developments relate to one another and to contemporary life.

This level of cognition is crucial for equipping future ministers and leaders. It enables them to articulate the faith in ways that are faithful and accessible, to teach others with clarity and depth, and to engage culture with both conviction and compassion. In the classroom, this may take the form of paraphrasing Scripture, explaining theological positions in dialogue with historical traditions, or drawing connections between doctrines and the lived experience of faith communities. Understanding is not static; it grows in depth and nuance through guided reflection, dialogue, and continual encounter with Scripture and tradition.

Artificial intelligence can serve this process when thoughtfully integrated into pedagogical practice. AI-driven tools can generate simplified summaries of complex texts, offer analogies or illustrations, and create visualizations of theological frameworks that clarify connections between ideas. These resources can assist students in moving from confusion to clarity, helping them engage with dense material in more digestible forms. However, true understanding is not merely the result of exposure to simplified content. It also requires wrestling with ambiguity, listening to the Spirit, and participating in the communal task of interpretation.

In theological education, understanding is a deeply spiritual act. It is the work of entering into the mystery of God's revelation and allowing that revelation to reshape one's assumptions, desires, and worldview. It is the fruit of attentiveness, guided inquiry, and patient engagement with the richness of the Christian tradition. When educators cultivate this kind of understanding in their students, they are helping form ministers who can faithfully interpret the gospel and proclaim its truth in a world hungry for meaning.

## Applying: Bridging Doctrine and Life

Application is the moment when theological knowledge moves from the page into practice. It is where abstract concepts meet lived reality, and where doctrine is translated into pastoral action, ethical decision-making, and embodied faith. In Bloom's Taxonomy, the application stage challenges students not just to understand theology, but to use it meaningfully in real-world contexts. For the seminary student, this often includes crafting sermons that speak to contemporary struggles, engaging in pastoral care that reflects theological integrity, or addressing complex moral dilemmas with biblical wisdom. This level of learning marks the transition from theory to praxis — where theology begins to live and breathe in the rhythms of ministry.

Applying theology requires discernment and imagination. It demands that students not only grasp what is true but also how that truth speaks into the complexity of human experience. Forgiveness must be applied in conflict mediation; doctrines of the imago Dei must shape pastoral care for the marginalized; ecclesiology must inform leadership practices. These are not exercises in abstraction, but acts of formation, grounded in the belief that theology is meant to be lived. The Incarnation itself — the Word made flesh — stands as the ultimate model of application. Jesus not only taught truth: He embodied it, inviting His followers to do the same.

Artificial intelligence, when wisely guided, can assist in this integrative work. AI platforms can simulate pastoral scenarios such as hospital visits, counseling sessions, or congregational conflicts, offering students a safe environment to test and refine their theological responses. Chat-based role-playing can facilitate practice in articulating faith in pastoral or evangelistic conversations. Tools that assist in sermon preparation can help students bridge the biblical text and the needs of a specific audience. Even AI-enhanced journaling tools can support students in connecting classroom learning with field education or ministry experiences. Used well, these technologies serve not as shortcuts but as aids for reflection and growth.

Ultimately, application is a deeply spiritual act — an expression of obedience, love, and service. It reflects the goal of theological education: not simply to produce thinkers, but to form wise and faithful practitioners of the gospel. When students can apply what they have learned with pastoral sensitivity, ethical integrity, and missional vision, theology becomes more than a discipline — it becomes a way of life.

## Analyzing: Seeing the Parts and the Whole

Analysis deepens theological learning by teaching students to examine structure, relationships, and assumptions. At this level of Bloom's Taxonomy, learners are not only receiving and applying theological content—they are beginning to interrogate it. Analysis involves identifying logical connections, exposing hidden presuppositions, differentiating between competing interpretations, and tracing the flow of theological arguments. Students learn to see the internal coherence (or lack thereof) within a doctrine, to compare frameworks across traditions, and to evaluate the integrity of interpretations considering Scripture and ecclesial teaching.

This skill is essential for cultivating discernment. In the New Testament, the apostle Paul exemplifies analytical thinking in his epistles, especially when contrasting the Old and New Covenants, unpacking Christological arguments, or carefully structuring theological exhortations. Likewise, theological students today must develop the capacity to compare patristic and Reformation soteriologies, critique cultural influences in contextual theologies, and map out theological movements across time. Analysis gives them the tools not only to understand theological content, but to ask how it has been shaped, what it assumes, and what implications it carries for life and ministry.

Artificial intelligence can aid this stage by offering conceptual comparison tools that contrast theological views, generating visual maps of arguments or biblical structures, and assisting in identifying semantic patterns across texts. For example, students might use AI to compare various atonement theories side-by-side, trace patterns in a Pauline letter, or visualize doctrinal themes across Church history. These tools can make the analytical process more accessible and even engaging, especially for visual learners.

Yet the work of analysis must remain grounded in theological wisdom. AI may highlight differences, but it cannot fully evaluate theological significance. It can present contrasts, but not context. For this reason, the educator's role is crucial in helping students ask the right questions and interpret their findings through a lens of biblical faithfulness and ecclesial accountability. Ultimately, analysis is not about dismantling theology but about understanding its architecture—so that students can build, critique, and reform in ways that honor the truth of the gospel and serve the life of the Church.

## Evaluating: Discernment and Theological Judgment

Evaluation marks a critical moment in the process of theological formation. It is the point at which students begin to exercise mature judgment—assessing the coherence, validity, and relevance of theological claims, ethical arguments, and ministerial practices. This level of Bloom's Taxonomy does not simply ask, "What does this mean?" or "How do I use it?" but "Is this true? Is it good? Is it faithful?" In this stage, learners develop the essential skill of discernment, what the early Church referred to as diakrisis—the ability to distinguish between truth and error, sound teaching and distortion, healthy practice and harmful misuse.

Theological evaluation involves engaging Scripture, tradition, reason, and experience in a dynamic conversation. Students must learn to weigh the credibility of sources, interrogate theological assumptions, and test ideas against the broader witness of the gospel. They must be able to critique not only doctrinal claims but also their practical outworkings in church life, public theology, and pastoral leadership.

Evaluation also extends to the character of ministry — asking not just whether something works, but whether it reflects the cruciform wisdom of Christ. It is not cynical or combative, but humble and faithful, seeking the flourishing of God's people.

Artificial intelligence can assist with this process by exposing students to contrasting theological viewpoints, prompting them to defend or refute ethical stances, and offering simulated peer review exercises. AI can suggest questions, generate examples, and even help create rubrics that support evaluative thinking. But it cannot make judgments of spiritual depth or moral weight. Discernment is cultivated not in isolation or through automation, but in the context of formation — in classrooms, churches, and communities where students are mentored in wisdom and shaped by love.

At its best, evaluation in theological education forms students into thoughtful, prayerful, and courageous leaders. These people are not swayed by every wind of doctrine, but who are able to shepherd others with clarity and conviction. In a world that often prizes efficiency over reflection and certainty over wisdom, theological educators must create space for careful, Spirit-guided evaluation. It is in this space that students learn not just what to believe, but how to think, how to listen, and how to lead with integrity and grace.

## Creating: Theological Imagination and Innovation

The highest level of Bloom's Taxonomy, creating, calls students to move beyond analysis and evaluation to synthesis and innovation. In theological education, this means that learners begin to construct something new out of what they have received: sermons that preach the gospel faithfully in their own voice, liturgies that speak to the context of a particular community, ministry strategies that respond to pressing pastoral or cultural needs, or even theological frameworks that address gaps or challenges in the tradition. Creating does not imply abandoning the past—it means engaging it with imaginative fidelity, drawing from the riches of Scripture and Church history to speak into the present with prophetic insight and pastoral creativity.

This stage represents a vital outcome of theological formation: the emergence of leaders who do not simply replicate what they have learned but contribute to the ongoing theological and missional witness of the Church. Students who create are not just reciting doctrines or echoing authors; they are prayerfully and theologically generating new expressions of Christian truth and practice that are both rooted and responsive. This could be seen in the composition of contextual liturgies, the development of new models for community engagement, the integration of theology with the arts, or the articulation of theological responses to emerging ethical issues. In all of this, creating reflects the Spirit's ongoing work to renew the Church and inspire fresh faithfulness in every generation.

Artificial intelligence may assist this level of learning by helping students brainstorm ideas, structure outlines, or synthesize sources in the early stages of creative work. For instance, AI might support a student in designing a curriculum, drafting a sermon framework, or exploring theological connections between disparate sources. When used in these ways, AI becomes a creative partner—offering suggestions without replacing the formative labor of theological imagination. Still, this process must remain firmly grounded in community, accountability, and the work of the Holy Spirit. Creativity in theology must be shaped by discernment, humility, and fidelity to the gospel story.

Creating, in the end, is not simply about producing content. It is about participation in God's redemptive work in the world. Theological educators are called to foster this kind of creativity—not as a capstone project, but as a vocation. The seminary classroom must be a space where students are empowered to imagine and articulate theology that builds up the Church, speaks truth to power, and offers hope to a broken world. In this space, the goal is not just that students learn theology, but that they become theologians: imaginative, courageous, and rooted in the love of Christ.

## Conclusion: A Framework for Flourishing

Bloom's Taxonomy offers theological educators a structure for designing courses that engage the full range of learning—intellectual, spiritual, and practical. When paired with formative pedagogy and thoughtful integration of digital tools, it becomes a powerful guide for shaping students into reflective practitioners, wise leaders, and creative theologians.

In a time when efficiency is prized over depth, and information over wisdom, Bloom's Taxonomy helps reclaim the slow, sacred work of formation. It reminds us that good teaching is not just about what students know, but who they become.

# Chapter 3
## Artificial Intelligence and the Future of Theological Teaching

### Introduction: Teaching at the Threshold of Technological Change

We are living at a pivotal moment in history — what some have called the fourth industrial revolution — marked by the rapid rise of artificial intelligence (AI). While technological shifts are not new to education or theology, the emergence of AI presents an unprecedented transformation in the way we think, communicate, and learn. For theological educators, this is not simply a question of classroom tools but a deeper issue of vocational response. How do we teach faithfully and wisely in an age when algorithms shape attention, and machines can generate sermons, summarize Scripture, and even mimic theological reasoning?

This chapter explores the changing landscape of education through the lens of AI and considers how theological educators can respond with discernment, creativity, and hope. It does not offer a simplistic embrace or rejection of AI, but a theological reflection on what is at stake — and what is possible — when teaching intersects with machine intelligence.

### What Is Artificial Intelligence?

Artificial intelligence (AI) refers to the development of computer systems capable of performing tasks that typically require human intelligence. These tasks include understanding language, recognizing patterns, making decisions, learning from experience, and even generating original content. At its core, AI is not a single technology but a broad field that encompasses machine learning, natural language processing, neural networks, and generative algorithms. These tools enable machines to mimic certain cognitive functions by processing vast amounts of data, identifying trends, and making predictions or suggestions based on that analysis.

In the realm of education, AI is increasingly present through tools such as adaptive learning platforms, virtual tutors, automated writing assistants, and interactive chatbots. These systems can tailor content to individual learners, provide instant feedback, simulate human conversation, and analyze student engagement and comprehension. For theological education specifically, AI may be used to summarize dense theological texts, provide structured outlines for complex arguments, or simulate conversations around ethical dilemmas. Students might interact with AI to test their understanding of historical theology or explore various interpretations of Scripture.

However, despite its sophistication, AI remains fundamentally limited. It operates through pattern recognition, statistical probabilities, and algorithmic training—not through wisdom, conscience, or spiritual insight. It can mimic human language, but it cannot comprehend divine mystery. It can assemble information, but it cannot embody discernment. Theological educators must therefore approach AI with a sober awareness of both its capabilities and its boundaries. While AI may assist in the process of learning, it is not a source of revelation, nor a substitute for the relational, prayerful, and Spirit-led nature of theological formation.

As AI continues to evolve, it will shape the contours of education and ministry. Yet theological educators are uniquely positioned to guide students in understanding not only what AI is and how it functions, but also how to relate to it ethically, spiritually, and theologically. This requires ongoing reflection on the nature of human identity, the meaning of wisdom, and the role of technology in the life of the Church.

## How AI Is Changing Education

The rise of artificial intelligence is transforming the landscape of education at every level. AI-powered tools are enabling forms of learning that were once unimaginable—providing personalized instruction, real-time feedback, and adaptive content delivery that respond to individual students' pace, interests, and performance. Educational platforms now use AI to track student engagement, identify areas of struggle, and suggest resources tailored to each learner's needs. For institutions with limited faculty or remote learners, these technologies offer new access to formative experiences that might otherwise be unavailable. In theological education, this means that students can engage in independent study with guided support, receive explanations of complex theological ideas, and even interact with simulations of pastoral conversations or historical theological debates.

However, the influence of AI also presents significant challenges to traditional pedagogical models. The ease with which students can generate essays, answer exam questions, or summarize texts with the help of AI tools raises serious questions about academic integrity and intellectual formation. There is a danger that students may come to rely on machines not as aids for reflection but as substitutes for the slow, embodied, and communal work of theological learning. Moreover, the educator's role is changing—from being the primary source of information to becoming a guide, curator, and interpreter in an environment saturated with intelligent systems. Teachers must now help students not only acquire knowledge but learn how to discern, evaluate, and interact responsibly with the tools that mediate that knowledge.

In this shifting landscape, theological educators must cultivate new forms of wisdom. They must remain grounded in their vocational identity as formers of persons, not just conveyors of content. Rather than resisting AI altogether or adopting it uncritically, educators are called to engage this technology with discernment — integrating its strengths while safeguarding the integrity of the learning process. This includes teaching students not just how to use AI tools, but how to reflect theologically on their use, recognizing the subtle ways in which technology shapes thought, relationship, and community. In doing so, theological education becomes a space not only of knowledge transfer but of moral and spiritual formation — preparing students to lead with wisdom in a world increasingly shaped by algorithms and automation.

## Risks and Challenges: Ethical, Pedagogical, and Theological

As artificial intelligence becomes more integrated into educational practice, it brings with it a host of complex risks and challenges that demand careful theological and ethical reflection. Ethically, the deployment of AI raises pressing concerns about authorship, data privacy, consent, and algorithmic bias. Students and educators alike must ask who owns the content generated by AI, how learning data is collected and used, and whether the systems reflect cultural, theological, or ideological biases embedded in their design. Without transparency and accountability, AI tools can inadvertently reinforce injustice, propagate misinformation, or erode trust in the educational process.

Pedagogically, there is the danger that AI could flatten the richness of theological learning into something transactional or mechanical. The temptation to automate instruction, grading, or content delivery may result in the loss of formative, dialogical, and communal elements that are essential to theological education. Theology is not merely the transfer of knowledge — it is a process of transformation that occurs in relationship, through conversation, and under the guidance of mentors who model the life of faith. If educators lean too heavily on AI systems, they risk replacing the living encounter with the dead logic of efficiency. This is especially true in disciplines like theology where nuance, silence, mystery, and affective presence matter just as much as information.

Theologically, perhaps the most profound challenge is the potential confusion between technological sophistication and spiritual depth. AI can generate convincing theological arguments, mimic pastoral language, or assemble complex doctrinal summaries. Yet it does so without belief, without prayer, and without the indwelling presence of the Holy Spirit. It cannot bear witness, offer pastoral care, or engage in spiritual discernment. Its "intelligence" is synthetic, and its voice is borrowed. If uncritically adopted, AI could foster an educational environment where theological truth is treated as data rather than as the lived wisdom of the Church. The human dimension of formation — mentoring, community, sacrament, and shared suffering — cannot be automated. This is particularly vital for preparing ministers, who must be shaped not only intellectually but spiritually and relationally.

These risks do not mean that AI has no place in theological education. But they do require that educators approach AI not merely as a convenience but as a tool that must be held in tension with the deeper purposes of formation. AI must serve pedagogy, not redefine it; it must support theological inquiry, not supplant spiritual formation. Above all, it must never displace the sacred responsibility of educators who walk alongside students as they grow in knowledge, faith, and love. The task is not simply to use AI responsibly, but to do so in ways that honor the humanity of learners and the divine calling of those who teach.

## Theological Integration: Teaching with AI, Not Teaching by AI

Faithful theological education in the age of artificial intelligence requires more than technical competence — it demands theological imagination. The task is not simply to incorporate AI into the classroom but to integrate it meaningfully into a vision of formation that remains rooted in the gospel, guided by the Spirit, and oriented toward the flourishing of the Church. Teaching with AI must never become teaching by AI. The distinction is crucial. AI may serve the learning process, but it must never be allowed to determine its goals, define its methods, or displace its relational and spiritual core.

To teach with AI theologically is to begin with the question of purpose: What are we trying to form in our students? What kind of people are we hoping they become? The goal of theological education is not merely comprehension or skill acquisition, but wisdom — shaped through the rhythms of Scripture, tradition, prayer, and community. AI can assist in this process by supporting tasks such as summarizing dense theological texts, generating study prompts, or offering feedback on writing. These contributions can help free educators to invest more deeply in mentoring, spiritual guidance, and reflective dialogue. When used judiciously, AI can enhance accessibility, personalize support, and enrich the learning journey.

However, the proper integration of AI also requires a reimagining of the educator's role. No longer merely a dispenser of information, the theological educator becomes a guide, shepherd, and curator of learning experiences. This shift invites greater intentionality in how learning environments are shaped, creating space for student reflection, peer conversation, and embodied practices of faith. Teachers will need to develop new discernment: not only how to use AI tools, but when not to use them, recognizing the irreplaceable value of human presence and pastoral engagement.

Students, likewise, must be formed not simply to use AI competently but to relate to it wisely. They need to learn to ask theological questions of the technologies they engage: What vision of the human person does this tool assume? How might it shape my understanding of knowledge, truth, or vocation? Educators must model this kind of theological inquiry by practicing both courage and caution—neither fearing innovation nor idolizing it. By doing so, they will form ministers and leaders who are equipped to navigate a rapidly changing world without losing sight of the deeper call to love God and neighbor.

In sum, the integration of AI into theological education must be purposeful, relational, and deeply theological. It must support—not replace—the formational practices that shape students into wise, humble, and Spirit-led servants of the Church. When used well, AI can become a tool not of control but of accompaniment, helping learners engage more deeply with the living tradition of the Church and the living God who calls them to serve.

## Conclusion: A Hopeful Vocation

Artificial intelligence is not going away. It will continue to reshape how we think, teach, and learn. The task for theological educators is not to retreat in fear nor rush ahead in naivete, but to walk forward in hope — grounded in Scripture, attuned to the Spirit, and responsive to the needs of the Church. AI is a tool; it is not a teacher. It can assist in the work of education, but it cannot replace the sacred vocation of forming people for gospel ministry.

As we stand at this threshold, we are called not simply to adopt new technologies, but to embody a new kind of wisdom — one that reflects the character of Christ, honors the complexity of human learning, and serves the redemptive mission of God in the world.

# Chapter 4
## Designing AI-Assisted Courses for Theological Formation

**Introduction: The Architecture of Theological Learning**

Designing courses in theological education is a sacred and strategic act—one that involves far more than selecting content or arranging assignments. It is the work of crafting formative pathways where students encounter not only theological ideas but the living God who calls them to ministry, discipleship, and witness. In this light, course design becomes a deep pastoral responsibility. The educator serves not just as a curriculum architect but as a spiritual guide, shaping spaces where theological inquiry and spiritual growth converge. Every decision—from learning outcomes to assessment practices—has the potential to either support or hinder the formation of wise, humble, and faithful leaders.

In the digital age, this responsibility takes on new dimensions. The rapid rise of artificial intelligence and digital tools challenges educators to reimagine how learning takes place and how formation is cultivated. Students increasingly engage in content asynchronously, interact through screens, and access knowledge via intelligent systems that respond to their needs in real-time. While these developments create new opportunities for accessibility and personalization, they also risk disembodying learning and reducing theological education to information delivery. Course design, therefore, must be deeply intentional attending to both the promise and the perils of technological integration.

Thoughtfully incorporating AI into course design is not about replacing human teachers or automating formation. Rather, it is about discerning how these tools might enhance the learning journey when used with pastoral care and theological integrity. The goal is not innovation for its own sake, but the creation of learning environments where students are drawn more deeply into Scripture, tradition, community, and calling. This chapter explores how educators can design AI-assisted theological courses that remain rooted in the mission of the Church, responsive to contemporary realities, and centered in the transformative power of the gospel.

## Framing Learning Outcomes Theologically

Learning outcomes serve as the compass of a course. They guide both educator and student by articulating what the learner should know, be able to do, and, in theological education, who they are becoming by the end of the journey. In secular academic settings, outcomes often emphasize knowledge acquisition and skill proficiency. But in theological education, learning outcomes must be shaped by a broader and deeper vision—one that includes spiritual formation, vocational clarity, and ecclesial service. They must reflect not only cognitive achievement but also the transformation of the heart, the deepening of faith, and the growth of pastoral and theological wisdom.

To frame learning outcomes theologically is to ask not only, "What should students learn?" but also, "What kind of people are we seeking to form?" Are we cultivating biblically rooted interpreters of Scripture? Ethically wise leaders? Compassionate pastors? Thoughtful theologians capable of discerning the movement of the Spirit in complex contexts? When learning outcomes are aligned with these formational goals, every aspect of the course — from content and pedagogy to assignments and assessment — becomes a means of spiritual and ministerial development.

In a digital age where artificial intelligence plays an increasing role in content delivery and engagement, it is especially important to be explicit about these theological goals. AI can accelerate information processing, provide content summaries, and even simulate conversations. But it cannot form character, shape virtue, or inspire a sense of calling. When educators clearly articulate learning outcomes that integrate knowledge, practice, and spiritual growth, they help ensure that AI serves formation rather than distorting it.

For example, an outcome might go beyond "Explain the doctrine of the Trinity" to "Articulate the doctrine of the Trinity and reflect on its implications for communal life and pastoral practice." Another might expand from "Understand ethical frameworks" to "Discern and apply ethical frameworks to real-life ministry dilemmas with pastoral sensitivity." These kinds of theologically rooted outcomes create room for AI tools to play a supportive role while keeping the primary focus on the human and divine dynamics at the heart of learning.

Ultimately, framing learning outcomes theologically is an act of hope. It expresses confidence that God is at work in the learning process, that students are not just information consumers but disciples in formation, and that education is one of the ways the Church participates in the ongoing work of equipping the saints for the mission of God in the world.

## Structuring Courses for Integration and Depth

The structure of a theological course is much more than a logistical framework—it is a formative rhythm that shapes the learner's experience over time. Just as liturgy provides a structure for worship that invites participation in God's story, so too does a well-designed course guide students through a journey of intellectual, spiritual, and ministerial growth. This journey must be intentional, grounded in the theological vision of the course, and paced in a way that supports both deep reflection and progressive mastery. The structure must move learners from foundational concepts toward more complex tasks such as critical analysis, contextual application, and creative theological synthesis.

An effective theological course should reflect the cognitive movement of Bloom's Taxonomy, building from remembering and understanding to applying, analyzing, evaluating, and ultimately creating. Each phase requires different kinds of engagement and support. Early in the course, students may need tools that help them access and organize core knowledge—such as overviews of historical theology, AI-generated timelines, or brief explanations of doctrinal terms. As students move toward more advanced stages, the structure should invite them to wrestle with complexity: exploring ethical case studies, engaging diverse theological perspectives, and integrating their learning with pastoral practice.

AI can be thoughtfully woven into this structure to support, but not dominate, the learning process. At foundational stages, AI tools might provide reading companions that help students grasp dense texts or generate visual aids that map theological frameworks. In middle phases, AI-driven role-play simulations can allow students to rehearse pastoral encounters or work through ministry dilemmas. In later stages, students might use AI to brainstorm sermon outlines, draft theological proposals, or collaborate on creative projects that respond to contemporary issues. The point is not to let AI dictate the structure, but to incorporate it in a way that enhances learning and supports spiritual reflection.

Equally important are moments that intentionally resist the speed and automation of AI. A theological course must include time and space for contemplation, prayer, peer dialogue, and embodied presence. Silence, lament, communal worship, and guided spiritual reflection are just as essential to the learning journey as textbooks or discussion boards. These practices root students in the incarnational reality of theological formation and serve as counterpoints to the disembodied nature of digital engagement.

Ultimately, structuring a theological course well is an act of pastoral care. It reflects a commitment to guide students through an integrated experience of knowing, being, and doing. By balancing the affordances of AI with the irreplaceable practices of community, reflection, and mentoring, educators can create courses that not only inform but transform — shaping learners who are equipped to serve the Church and the world with wisdom, humility, and imagination.

## Designing Assessments with Integrity and Imagination

Assessment is not merely a way to measure what students have learned — it is an opportunity to invite them into deeper engagement, reflection, and synthesis. In theological education, assessments serve a dual purpose: they evaluate academic competence and foster spiritual and ministerial growth. To be effective, assessments must align with the theological and formational goals of the course. They should do more than test memory or reward formulaic answers; they should challenge students to integrate their learning, reflect critically, and embody theological wisdom in real-world contexts.

The rise of AI presents both a challenge and an opportunity in assessment design. On the one hand, the ease with which students can generate AI-assisted responses raises questions about authorship, originality, and intellectual integrity. On the other, AI can serve as a companion in formative assessment, offering low-stakes feedback, helping students rehearse arguments, or providing tools for exploring pastoral scenarios. The educator's task is to ensure that assessments are not easily outsourced to machines but instead require human insight, spiritual discernment, and contextual application.

One approach is to design assessments that are deeply personalized and contextual. For example, rather than asking students to write a generic essay on atonement theories, an instructor might ask them to reflect on how those theories shape their approach to pastoral care in trauma-informed ministry. Instead of issuing multiple-choice quizzes, educators can assign theological reflections on current events, sermon outlines for communities, or case studies that require ethical discernment grounded in Scripture and tradition. These types of assessments resist automation and foster embodied theological thinking.

AI can play a supportive role in this process. It might be used to generate mock scenarios for student analysis, offer grammatical or structural feedback on drafts, or help students visualize theological concepts in comparative form. However, summative evaluations — those that determine final mastery — should remain rooted in human engagement and spiritual discernment. Educators might include oral examinations, peer-to-peer feedback, or spiritual autobiographies that reflect the student's journey through the course.

Moreover, integrating reflective practices into assessment can increase both accountability and depth. Students might be asked to describe how they used AI tools in the learning process, what they learned through that interaction, and how it shaped their understanding of theology, ministry, or ethics. This kind of metacognitive reflection helps cultivate transparency and encourages students to think theologically not only about their subject matter but about their use of technology itself.

In the end, assessment in theological education is an extension of the educator's calling: to form, not merely to grade; to equip, not merely to evaluate. By designing assessments that are imaginative, rigorous, and spiritually grounded, educators help students become not just better thinkers, but more faithful disciples and discerning leaders.

## Supporting Spiritual and Ministerial Formation

At the heart of theological education is the sacred work of formation—cultivating not only informed minds but transformed lives. While academic knowledge and critical thinking are essential, they are insufficient without the development of spiritual maturity, pastoral sensitivity, and vocational clarity. In every course, educators must intentionally create space for students to grow in their relationship with God, deepen their call to ministry, and engage in practices that nurture wisdom, humility, and love for others. This task becomes even more urgent in an age where digital tools, including AI, can easily dominate the learning environment and displace embodied practices of formation.

To support spiritual and ministerial formation, course design must weave together theological reflection and lived discipleship. This involves structuring opportunities for prayer, guided spiritual exercises, community worship, and vocational discernment. It includes assignments that call students to reflect on their own spiritual lives, consider the pastoral implications of what they are learning, and engage with mentors, peers, and local faith communities. Field education, spiritual direction, small group dialogue, and immersion experiences remain essential, anchoring students in the relational and incarnational dimensions of Christian ministry.

The integration of AI into the learning environment introduces both opportunities and tensions. On one hand, AI can assist with practical tasks — offering summaries of spiritual texts, facilitating journaling prompts, or simulating pastoral conversations for practice and critique. It can also expand access to theological resources for students in isolated or underserved contexts. On the other hand, AI cannot replicate the sacred work of spiritual formation. It cannot pray with a student, offer compassionate presence in suffering, or discern the movement of the Spirit in a moment of crisis. It cannot teach students how to listen deeply, bear burdens, or love across differences. These practices must be embodied, relational, and rooted in the rhythms of the Church.

Therefore, in AI-assisted courses, educators must be especially vigilant to ensure that digital engagement does not eclipse spiritual attentiveness. Assignments and course rhythms should draw students back into silence, into Scripture, into conversation with others, and into the presence of God. They should ask not only "What did I learn?" but "How is God forming me through this learning?" and "What kind of leader am

I becoming?" Formation is not a byproduct of education—it is the goal. And that goal must remain central, even amid technological change.

In short, theological educators must act as spiritual guides, not just content designers. They must model the habits of the soul they hope to cultivate in their students and design courses that foster trust, vulnerability, reflection, and transformation. When AI is used with discernment and humility—alongside embodied practices of faith—it can support, rather than hinder, the deep work of becoming more like Christ for the sake of the world.

## Conclusion: A Course is a Formation Pathway

A theological course is never merely an academic exercise. It is a sacred space where minds are sharpened, hearts are stirred, and callings are clarified. Each course offers a pathway—an intentional structure through which students are invited to grow in wisdom, deepen their love for God, and prepare for faithful service in the world. Designing such a course is not a task to be taken lightly; it is an act of spiritual architecture. The educator builds not just a syllabus, but a context for encounter—with Scripture, tradition, community, and the living Christ.

In a world increasingly shaped by artificial intelligence, course design must rise to the challenge of integrating new tools without losing the essence of theological formation. AI can assist educators and enrich student experiences, but it must always remain a servant, never the master. It may enhance learning, provide accessibility, and support engagement, but it cannot replace the formative power of human presence, pastoral mentorship, and communal discernment. Educators must carefully and prayerfully curate their courses to ensure that technology serves the mission — not distracts from it.

A well-designed theological course does more than deliver content; it forms character. It invites students not only to think critically but to live faithfully. It challenges them to bring theology into dialogue with their own stories, their communities, and the needs of the world. This kind of course requires deep intentionality — attention to learning outcomes that shape both mind and heart, structures that support depth and reflection, assessments that call forth integration and creativity, and rhythms that prioritize spiritual and ministerial formation.

In the end, theological education is a journey of transformation. Each course is a step on that journey, and the way it is designed matters profoundly. As we navigate new technological frontiers, we must do so with the conviction that formation — real, Spirit-led, Christ-centered formation — cannot be automated. It must be cultivated, nurtured, and guarded. And it is in this sacred responsibility that theological educators find their deepest calling: to shape not only what students know, but who they become.

## Chapter 5
## *Cultivating AI Literacy in Theological Students and Faculty*

### Introduction: Discipleship in a Digital Age

We are living in a moment of profound technological transformation. Artificial intelligence is no longer the domain of distant research labs or speculative science fiction—it is embedded in our everyday lives. It shapes how we communicate, search for information, shop, study, and even pray. In this digital age, where algorithms increasingly mediate our engagement with the world, the Church must respond not only with awareness, but with theological depth and pastoral wisdom. Theological education stands at a critical crossroads: either it will prepare students and faculty to engage these changes thoughtfully, or it will risk becoming irrelevant to the real challenges of ministry and formation in the twenty-first century.

AI literacy has become an essential part of theological formation, not simply as a technical skill but as a new dimension of discipleship. Students preparing for ministry must be equipped to understand how AI affects human behavior, relationships, and even spiritual practices. They must be able to discern when AI can serve ministry purposes—and when it may distort them. Likewise, faculty must be prepared to guide students through this shifting terrain, integrating theological tradition with contemporary technological realities. In both cases, the goal is not mastery of tools alone but the cultivation of wisdom: the kind of wisdom that recognizes what it means to be human in a world increasingly shaped by machines.

This chapter addresses the urgent need to cultivate AI literacy in theological institutions. It explores what AI literacy looks like in theological contexts, why discernment must guide its use, how it can be woven into the curriculum, and what kinds of faculty development and institutional vision are needed to sustain this work. The integration of AI into theological education is not about keeping up with trends—it is about forming leaders who can faithfully serve the Church in a world profoundly shaped by technology. Ultimately, this is a chapter about formation: forming thoughtful, ethical, and spiritually grounded individuals who can think critically and lead courageously in the digital age.

## Defining AI Literacy for Theological Contexts

Artificial intelligence literacy, when understood through a theological lens, must go far beyond technical competence. It is not merely the ability to use AI tools effectively or to navigate digital platforms with confidence. Instead, AI literacy in theological education involves the capacity to think theologically about the presence and power of AI in our lives, to reflect critically on its cultural and ethical implications, and to engage with it in ways that are grounded in the wisdom of the Christian tradition. In short, AI literacy is a form of theological discernment—rooted in a robust understanding of human dignity, vocation, and the purposes of education and ministry.

In this context, AI literacy includes the ability to ask foundational questions: How does AI shape our understanding of knowledge, community, and authority? What assumptions does it make about what it means to be human? How might its use influence spiritual practices, pastoral care, or ecclesial relationships? These are not abstract concerns. They are deeply relevant to students preparing for the lives of ministry and scholarship in a world where AI already influences how people search for meaning, relate to one another, and even interpret Scripture. AI literacy, therefore, equips students not only to function in a digital world but to lead within it—offering a thoughtful, faithful, and critical Christian presence.

For students, AI literacy means developing the ability to use AI tools wisely and ethically in contexts such as sermon preparation, theological writing, research, and ministry planning. It means knowing when AI can serve a purpose—such as summarizing a dense theological text or simulating a pastoral counseling scenario—and when its use may undermine the learning process or pastoral relationship. For faculty, AI literacy entails the ability to design courses that model responsible engagement, evaluate student work considering AI's capabilities, and reflect on how digital technologies intersect with theological content and pedagogy.

At all levels, AI literacy must be anchored in a theological vision of human beings as creatures made in the image of God—called to steward knowledge, practice discernment, and embody love in community. It must be shaped by doctrines of creation, incarnation, and eschatology that remind us that wisdom is not algorithmic, that truth is more than data, and that formation happens in the presence of others and before God. Without this grounding, AI literacy risks becoming a mere technical proficiency rather than a means of spiritual maturity and ethical engagement.

## Teaching Discernment, Not Just Technique

In theological education, the aim is never simply to convey technical proficiency — it is to cultivate discernment. The same must be true when it comes to artificial intelligence. Teaching students and faculty how to use AI is important, but insufficient on its own. The greater task is to help them develop the wisdom to know when and why to use AI, and when and why to refrain. Discernment in this context is not about fear or rejection, nor about uncritical enthusiasm. It is about attentiveness to the ways technology shapes human thought, behavior, and community, and about aligning our use of AI with the values of the gospel and the purposes of theological formation.

AI invites efficiency, speed, and convenience. But the life of faith often calls for slowness, attentiveness, and vulnerability. Educators must therefore guide students in asking deeper questions: What does it mean to learn with integrity in an age of instant answers? How do I remain present to God and others when I am constantly tempted by digital shortcuts? When I use AI to generate a sermon outline or theological summary, am I using it to enhance my work — or am I avoiding the difficult, prayerful wrestling that true learning often requires?

Such questions cannot be answered with a list of dos and don'ts. They must be explored through habits of reflection, community dialogue, and guided experimentation. Classroom practices such as theological reflection essays, structured conversations about the ethics of AI use, or communal commitments to honest authorship can provide space for this kind of discernment. Educators can also model transparency by narrating their own learning journey with AI — sharing where they have found it helpful, where they remain cautious, and how they are wrestling with its theological implications.

Discernment is also shaped by spiritual practice. Prayer, Scripture reading, silence, and worship all form the inner life from which wise engagement with technology flows. Without these practices, the use of AI — even in theological settings — can quickly become disembodied and disconnected from the very truths it is meant to serve. But when students and faculty are grounded in prayerful reflection and a communal pursuit of truth, they are better equipped to evaluate the influence of AI on their thinking, relationships, and ministry.

Ultimately, teaching discernment means cultivating a particular kind of posture, posture of humility, curiosity, and responsibility. It means forming leaders who are not only capable of using technology, but who are also courageous enough to question it, wise enough to limit it, and imaginative enough to redirect it toward ends that glorify God and serve the Church. AI may offer tools, but it is discernment that ensures those tools serve rather than shape us.

## Building AI Literacy into the Curriculum

AI literacy in theological education cannot be confined to an elective course or a one-off seminar. If it is to form Christian leaders who are equipped to minister in a world increasingly shaped by artificial intelligence, it must be thoughtfully integrated across the curriculum. This integration involves more than offering technical training — it requires embedding theological reflection on AI within the core disciplines of biblical studies, theology, ethics, pastoral care, and practical ministry. AI literacy becomes most formative when it is connected to the very heart of what theological education seeks to do: to prepare wise, discerning, Spirit-led leaders for the Church and the world.

In biblical studies, students can explore how AI-assisted translation tools compare to traditional interpretive methods, raising questions about the nature of textual authority, meaning, and cultural nuance. In theology courses, they can examine how doctrines of the image of God, incarnation, or eschatology speak into our understanding of machine intelligence and human distinctiveness. In courses on ethics, students might wrestle with issues of bias, surveillance, data ethics, and the social impacts of AI on marginalized communities. In pastoral care or counseling classes, they can engage with emerging AI-based tools for mental health support, asking what it means to care for souls in an age of algorithms.

Homiletics and spiritual formation classes also offer fertile ground. Students can reflect on the use of AI in sermon preparation, evaluating its strengths and limitations — and develop practices for maintaining authenticity, prayerfulness, and pastoral integrity when digital tools are involved. Formation classes might guide students in journaling about their relationship with technology, naming how it affects their prayer life, their sense of presence, and their understanding of vocation. These conversations should not be compartmentalized. They should be continuous, contextual, and connected to the lived experience of the Church in the digital age.

This level of curricular integration requires collaboration. Faculty across disciplines must work together to identify shared goals, develop interdisciplinary modules, and create space for students to connect their learning across different areas of study. Partnerships with departments of philosophy, communication, or computer science (where available) can enrich these efforts, offering critical insight into the mechanics of AI while maintaining the centrality of theological and pastoral reflection.

Ultimately, building AI literacy into the curriculum is an act of stewardship. It acknowledges that theological education is preparing students not for the world that once was, but for the world that is and will be. By weaving AI-related inquiry into the full tapestry of theological education, institutions can form leaders who are not only technologically informed, but theologically grounded — capable of leading the Church with creativity, courage, and wisdom in an era of rapid change.

## Supporting Faculty Development and Institutional Vision

The integration of AI into theological education cannot succeed without the intentional development of faculty. Professors are not only content experts and classroom facilitators, but they are also spiritual guides and institutional leaders whose approach to technology deeply influences how students engage with it. Yet many faculty members find themselves underprepared or hesitant when it comes to artificial intelligence. For some, the rapid pace of technological change creates uncertainty; for others, concerns about academic integrity, theological coherence, or spiritual formation provoke resistance. Institutions must respond not with pressure, but with support — creating space for faculty to learn, explore, and reflect within a framework that is both intellectually rigorous and theologically grounded.

Faculty development around AI should not be limited to technical training, though that is certainly needed. More importantly, it should include time and resources for theological inquiry, collaborative experimentation, and vocational reflection. Workshops that bring faculty together across disciplines to discuss AI's implications for pedagogy and pastoral formation can foster shared insight and mutual encouragement. Sabbaticals or research grants can empower faculty to investigate AI's role in their own field and develop innovative approaches for classroom integration. Peer learning groups and interdisciplinary dialogues can nurture a culture of curiosity and courage, replacing fear with faithful engagement.

At the same time, faculty development must be situated within a broader institutional vision. AI literacy should not be an individual project or the interest of a few innovators—it must be embraced as a shared commitment that flows from the mission of the theological school. This vision begins with leadership. Presidents, deans, and academic committees must articulate how the school's theological identity informs its posture toward technology. Is the institution committed to cultivating discernment in a digital age? Does it see AI as a tool to support formation, or as a threat to be managed? What theological values will shape its policies on AI usage, data ethics, academic honesty, and digital pedagogy?

These questions must be answered not in isolation, but in community. Institutions should involve students, alumni, pastors, and board members in these conversations, ensuring that the policies and practices that emerge are grounded in lived ministry experience as well as theological reflection. Clear guidelines around the use of AI in coursework, expectations for attribution and authorship, and standards for integrity and justice in the adoption of new tools should be developed transparently and revisited regularly. These policies must not be merely restrictive—they should be formative, helping students and faculty alike grow in wisdom, integrity, and theological imagination.

Supporting faculty in this work is not only a matter of professional development, but also a matter of institutional fidelity. If theological education is to remain responsive, prophetic, and transformational in the age of artificial intelligence, its educators must be equipped and empowered to lead the way. Faculty are the bridge between tradition and innovation, and institutions that invest in their flourishing will be better prepared to serve the Church in the years to come.

## Conclusion: Wisdom for a New Era

As artificial intelligence reshapes the contours of our cultural, social, and intellectual landscape, theological education stands at a defining moment. The Church does not have the luxury of indifference or delay; it must respond with thoughtful engagement, ethical clarity, and theological conviction. AI literacy is not simply about preparing students and faculty to survive in a technologically saturated world, it is about equipping them to lead with wisdom, courage, and integrity. It is about forming people who can navigate the digital age with spiritual discernment, who can distinguish between the tools that serve the gospel and those that subtly undermine it, and who can model an alternative way of being—rooted in communion, justice, and hope.

This kind of training cannot be reduced to a skill set or checklist. It requires a holistic vision of discipleship, one that integrates technology into the broader horizon of God's redemptive purposes. AI literacy, at its best, helps students and educators see with new eyes—recognizing where AI enhances ministry and learning, where it threatens to deform our practices, and where it calls for prophetic resistance. It fosters humility in the face of complexity, courage in the face of change, and creativity in the face of automation.

Most of all, it nurtures faithfulness—faithfulness to God's call, to the mission of the Church, and to the formation of communities marked by love and truth.

In this sense, AI literacy is not an optional add-on to theological education. It is a dimension of our calling to make disciples who can teach, preach, counsel, and lead in the real world—this world—where algorithms already influence how people think, learn, and relate. If we do not form students to engage in this world theologically, we risk sending them into ministry unprepared and unequipped. But if we do, if we teach them to reflect critically, live ethically, and think theologically about AI, we will be helping to shape leaders who can embody the gospel in a world AI is helping to create.

The future of theological education depends on such leaders—leaders who can teach with wisdom, pastor with discernment, and bear witness with grace. In forming them, we take part in the Spirit's work of preparing the Church for what lies ahead. That is not a technical task. It is a deeply theological one. And it begins with a renewed commitment to truth, love, and the wise, Spirit-filled use of every tool entrusted to us, for the glory of God and the good of the world.

# Chapter 6
## AI Tools and Strategies for Lower-Order Thinking Skills

**Introduction**

In theological education, the cultivation of intellectual and spiritual depth depends on a firm grasp of foundational knowledge. Before students can analyze doctrines, apply Scripture to ministry, or evaluate theological arguments, they must first develop a working command of basic terms, texts, and categories. These lower order thinking skills, particularly remembering and understanding, provide the essential building blocks for more complex learning. They are not merely preparatory stages to be rushed through, but essential dimensions of learning that provide the scaffolding for critical thinking, spiritual formation, and faithful ministry.

Artificial intelligence offers new opportunities to support these lower order thinking processes. In an age when students are inundated with information, AI tools can provide clarity, structure, and personalized reinforcement. AI can help students recall key theological terms, practice Scripture memory, summarize challenging texts, and visualize doctrinal relationships. When used thoughtfully, these technologies can alleviate some of the cognitive load that accompanies introductory theological study.

This chapter explores how AI can support the development of lower order thinking skills in theological education. It focuses on two critical domain-remembering and understanding—and describes how emerging tools such as ChatGPT, AI-powered flashcard and quiz generators, and intelligent glossaries can be used to enhance learning. While these tools offer exciting possibilities, they must be implemented with pedagogical wisdom and theological intentionality. AI is not a replacement for disciplined study, but a companion that, when guided by thoughtful educators, can reinforce learning, spark curiosity, and lay the groundwork for deeper theological reflection.

## Remembering: Using AI to Review Theological Terms, Texts, and Memory Aids

The cognitive skill of remembering is foundational in theological education, encompassing the ability to recall essential facts, terms, and texts. It forms the basis for everything else that follows in theological reasoning and ministerial practice. Students must learn the vocabulary of the tradition — words like atonement, incarnation, and eschatology — as well as key Scripture passages, historical dates, theological figures, and doctrinal formulations. Far from being a rote or mechanical exercise, the act of remembering in theological education is a deeply formative practice that enables students to inhabit the language of faith, recall the narrative of Scripture, and root their thinking in the shared memory of the Church.

Artificial intelligence offers powerful assistance in helping students internalize this foundational knowledge. Generative AI tools like ChatGPT can produce customized flashcards, quizzes, or keyword explanations aligned with a course syllabus or textbook. A student preparing for a church history exam, for example, can input a study guide into an AI tool and receive a tailored review session, complete with sample definitions, short-answer questions, and memory prompts. AI can also produce practice tests and adaptive quizzes that challenge students to recall key information under timed conditions, helping them build confidence and fluency in preparation for exams or ministry settings.

In addition to linguistic recall, AI can support the memorization of biblical passages and liturgical texts. It can simulate repetitive recall, test recognition through question banks, and even use spaced repetition systems — an evidence-based technique to reinforce long-term memory retention. By tracking what a student consistently remembers versus what they repeatedly forget, these tools can optimize study time and increase confidence.

Importantly, remembering in theological education is never an end. It is always in service of deeper understanding, interpretation, and formation. AI, when used well, can support this process by reinforcing knowledge through active engagement rather than passive review. Yet it is the educator who frames the purpose: not merely to pass a test, but to hold the language and story of the faith in one's mind and heart. Remembering sacred texts and theological terms is part of being shaped by the Christian tradition, allowing students to internalize its language, rehearse its truths, and participate more fully in the life and witness of the Church.

### Understanding: Generative AI for Basic Summaries, Flashcards, Concept Mapping

Understanding, as the second level of Bloom's taxonomy, builds upon the foundation of memory by enabling students to grasp meaning, interpret content, and express theological ideas in their own words. In a theological context, understanding means more than simply knowing terms or dates — it involves being able to explain what those terms signify, how they relate to one another, and why they matter for faith and ministry. Students must learn to articulate the implications of doctrines, paraphrase complex theological concepts, and connect scriptural narratives to broader theological themes. This level of comprehension is essential for fruitful engagement in classroom dialogue, faithful preaching, and informed pastoral leadership.

Generative AI tools can support the process of understanding by offering immediate, interactive ways to break down difficult material. A student might use ChatGPT to summarize a dense reading from Augustine or Barth into more accessible language, or to explain the relationship between justification and sanctification in different theological traditions. The act of prompting an AI model to generate a summary, and then evaluating its clarity and accuracy, reinforces comprehension by forcing students to identify what they do and do not yet understand. This interaction can be iterative, as students refine their prompts or ask follow-up questions to deepen their grasp of the subject.

AI is also particularly effective in creating visual tools that promote comprehension. Concept mapping, for instance, allows students to see how ideas interrelate, forming a mental framework that is especially helpful when navigating unfamiliar theological terrain. AI can assist in generating these maps automatically, clustering themes such as attributes of God, stages of redemptive history, or connections between doctrines across denominational lines. Flashcards, too, become more powerful when generated dynamically by AI, tailored to a student's needs and organized around thematic groupings rather than just isolated facts.

While AI can facilitate understanding, it cannot substitute for the kind of deep learning that comes through spiritual reflection, class discussion, and communal exploration. Theological comprehension involves not only intellectual clarity but also spiritual attentiveness — an openness to mystery, complexity, and the leading of the Spirit. Therefore, AI must be used not to shortcut understanding but to scaffold it: to help students build the confidence and conceptual clarity they need to go deeper in their theological journey. Used in this way, AI becomes a tool not of simplification but of illumination, guiding learners toward greater insight and deeper conviction.

## Tools: ChatGPT, AI Quiz Generators, AI-Enabled Glossaries

A range of artificial intelligence tools are now available to support lower-order thinking skills in theological education, and their thoughtful application can significantly enhance student learning. Among the most prominent is ChatGPT, a generative AI model capable of producing coherent and contextually responsive text. Students can use ChatGPT to clarify definitions of theological terms, generate example flashcards based on course content, or summarize key ideas from readings. Because the tool can tailor its responses to specific prompts, it allows learners to engage material at their own pace and level of comprehension. For instance, a first-year seminarian encountering Christological terminology for the first time can ask ChatGPT to define "hypostatic union" in simple terms, while a more advanced student might request a comparison of Eastern and Western interpretations of that doctrine.

AI quiz generators represent another powerful resource. These tools allow educators and students to input a passage, reading, or term list and generate a variety of quiz formats — multiple choice, fill-in-the-blank, true/false, and even short answer questions. By encouraging frequent low-stakes testing, AI quiz generators help reinforce memory and boost confidence. Moreover, because they can be regenerated with new questions each time, they offer endless opportunities for review and practice without becoming repetitive. Instructors can use these quizzes to support flipped classroom models or to provide formative assessments that pinpoint areas of confusion before summative evaluations.

AI-enabled glossaries offer a third avenue of support. These digital tools combine traditional vocabulary lists with interactive, AI-supported features such as contextual usage examples, voice pronunciation, and real-time visualizations. For theological education, this means students can engage doctrinal, biblical, and historical terminology in a multidimensional way — seeing how terms are used in different theological systems, connecting them to Scripture passages, or tracking how their meanings have evolved over time. Such tools can be embedded into course websites or learning management systems, allowing students to explore terms as they encounter them in lectures or readings.

While each of these tools is valuable on their own, their greatest potential lies in how they are integrated into the learning environment. Used intentionally, they can free cognitive space for students to focus on understanding rather than simply organizing content. They allow for personalized review strategies that respect different learning styles and levels of preparedness. Yet, these tools must always be framed by the educator's larger pedagogical and theological vision. The goal is not simply to make learning easier, but to make it more meaningful — to support the student's journey toward becoming a theologically literate, spiritually grounded, and pastorally wise leader.

## Conclusion

Lower order thinking skills may appear basic, but they are essential to the architecture of theological education. Without the ability to remember key terms, understand central doctrines, and recognize foundational patterns, students are unequipped to engage the more complex demands of theological reflection, ethical evaluation, and pastoral application. These early stages of learning are where theological literacy begins — where language is formed, frameworks are internalized, and the intellectual soil is tilled for deeper growth.

Artificial intelligence, when harnessed wisely, can serve as a faithful ally in this formative process. It offers personalized, scalable, and dynamic tools that can support student learning across a wide range of content areas and educational backgrounds. From flashcard generation and interactive glossaries to quiz creation and conceptual mapping, AI can reduce cognitive overload, enhance comprehension, and free up class time for richer engagement. Yet, its real value emerges not from its efficiency, but from how it is embedded within a pedagogy of formation — one that values wisdom over speed, integrity over automation, and relationship over convenience.

As theological educators and institutions continue to explore the role of AI, they must do so with discernment, ensuring that these tools serve rather than shape their vision of learning. AI should never be a shortcut that bypasses the hard work of study, memory, and engagement. Instead, it should be a companion — supporting students as they encounter the beauty, complexity, and challenge of the Christian tradition.

When framed by theological purpose and used with pastoral sensitivity, AI can help students lay the groundwork for a lifelong journey of faithful learning, ministry, and discipleship.

# Chapter 7
## AI in Developing Higher-Order Thinking Skills

**Introduction**

Higher-order thinking skills lie at the heart of theological education. These skills — applying, analyzing, evaluating, and creating — move students beyond the absorption of knowledge into active engagement with theological ideas and ministry contexts. They represent a shift from what is known to what can be done with that knowledge: applying it to real-life situations, discerning patterns and tensions within theological systems, weighing arguments with critical judgment, and producing new expressions of faith that are contextually grounded, theologically coherent, and pastorally sensitive.

In an era shaped by artificial intelligence, these higher-order skills remain more important than ever. While AI excels at storing information and generating content, it cannot replace the human faculties of moral discernment, spiritual wisdom, or ecclesial responsibility. Theological educators must therefore not only preserve these skills but find new ways to nurture them. AI can be a powerful tool in this endeavor when employed thoughtfully. It can simulate pastoral challenges, offer comparative theological insights across traditions, and provide prompts that stimulate reflection and debate.

This chapter explores how AI can support the development of higher order thinking in theological students. Each section focuses on one cognitive domain from Bloom's taxonomy—application, analysis, evaluation, and creation—demonstrating how AI can function as a scaffold for deeper engagement rather than a substitute for human thought. Alongside these possibilities, the chapter also addresses important cautions around authorship, integrity, and the formative role of theological education. As we embrace the possibilities AI offers, we must do so with a clear commitment to formation, ensuring that technological tools serve—not replace—the deeply human, spiritual, and communal work of theological education.

## Applying: Using AI to Simulate Pastoral Situations or Hermeneutical Tasks

The application of knowledge is where theological learning begins to touch the lived experience of ministry. It is not enough for students to recite doctrines or interpret texts—they must learn how to embody theological insights in practical, pastoral settings. Whether navigating ethical dilemmas, addressing congregational crises, or preaching the gospel into complex cultural contexts, students must be able to take what they have studied and apply it with wisdom, compassion, and contextual awareness. This is the moment where theology moves from abstraction to action.

Artificial intelligence can serve as a helpful companion in cultivating this ability. AI tools can simulate pastoral encounters—such as a hospital visit, a conflict resolution meeting, or a conversation about grief—allowing students to rehearse their theological and pastoral responses. These simulations offer low-stakes opportunities to practice difficult conversations and receive constructive feedback. A student might interact with an AI-powered role-play scenario in which they counsel a congregant wrestling with a moral decision, a theological doubt, or a personal tragedy, prompting the student to draw upon Scripture, doctrine, and pastoral wisdom to respond with care and clarity. Similarly, AI can support hermeneutical applications by helping students work through various interpretive lenses. For instance, a student could input a biblical passage and request summaries or interpretive perspectives from liberation theology, feminist theology, or historical-critical approaches. These AI-generated responses offer points of comparison that students must engage critically discerning what is helpful, what is lacking, and how different hermeneutical methods shape meaning. This not only sharpens their interpretive skills but also deepens their awareness of how theology functions contextually, shaping both understanding and practice in diverse ministry settings.

However, while AI can assist in simulating situations and offering interpretive diversity, it cannot replace the deeper spiritual and pastoral discernment that real ministry requires. True application involves more than choosing the right answer — it requires presence, empathy, listening, and love. Educators must ensure that AI remains a tool that supports formation, not one that mimics it. When guided by a strong pedagogical framework, AI can help students bridge doctrine and life, developing the skill to discern how theological convictions translate into wise action in varied and often unpredictable ministry contexts.

## Analyzing: Comparing Doctrinal Systems with AI Analysis Tools

Analysis invites students to move beyond simply applying theological knowledge to breaking it down examining its structure, assumptions, implications, and interconnections. This level of thinking is crucial in theological education, where doctrines are not merely learned but evaluated for coherence, biblical grounding, and historical development. Students must be trained to ask not just what a theologian believes, but why, how those beliefs are formed, and what difference they make. Analysis reveals the underlying frameworks that shape theological claims, exposing the presuppositions, internal logic, and implications that often remain hidden beneath the surface of a doctrine or argument.

Artificial intelligence offers compelling tools to support this level of engagement. Students can use AI to compare doctrinal systems side by side, exploring how various theologians, traditions, or historical movements approach central themes such as Christology, soteriology, or ecclesiology. With natural language processing and semantic analysis capabilities, AI can highlight key distinctions in terminology, structure, emphasis, and even tone. For example, a student comparing Reformed and Wesleyan theologies might use AI to generate summaries of each tradition's view on sanctification, highlighting how the Reformed emphasis on divine sovereignty contrasts with the Wesleyan focus on human cooperation in the process of holiness.

AI can also assist students in visually mapping theological arguments, helping them trace how ideas unfold across different texts or traditions. These visualizations clarify the relationships between theological concepts — such as how anthropology impacts Christology, or how eschatology shapes ecclesial mission. By breaking complex systems into parts and examining how those parts fit together, students begin to see theology not as a set of isolated beliefs but as a dynamic, interconnected framework. AI, when used thoughtfully, can illuminate these patterns and relationships, providing students with a clearer grasp of theological complexity and a stronger foundation for critical engagement.

However, it is crucial that AI remain a tool for guidance and not a substitute for theological reasoning. Analysis in theology is not a purely mechanical or computational task—it is shaped by context, tradition, and the interpretive communities that form our ways of knowing. Students must learn to bring their own questions, experiences, and theological commitments to the analytical process. Used appropriately, AI can help students develop these muscles of discernment, sharpening their ability to identify underlying assumptions, trace theological reasoning, and articulate informed critiques of complex doctrinal systems.

## Evaluating: Critiquing Theological Arguments with AI Support

Evaluation is one of the most vital capacities theological education seeks to cultivate. It involves the ability to make informed judgments about the coherence, credibility, and implications of theological arguments, ethical frameworks, and ministry strategies. This level of thinking calls for critical reflection rooted not in skepticism but in diakrisis—spiritual discernment that weighs truth claims considering Scripture, tradition, reason, and experience. Students must learn to assess not only whether a theological claim is logically consistent or biblically supported, but also whether it is pastorally responsible, historically grounded, and reflective of the character of God.

Artificial intelligence can serve as a partner in developing evaluative skills by exposing students to a range of perspectives on a theological question and inviting them to assess those views considering their convictions and tradition. For example, a student studying the doctrine of atonement could prompt an AI tool to outline multiple views—penal substitution, Christus Victor, moral influence—and then engage in evaluating their biblical support, pastoral implications, and theological coherence. Such engagement encourages the student to weigh not only the doctrinal content of each view, but also how these interpretations might shape preaching, discipleship, and the lived experience of the gospel in different contexts.

In addition to comparative analysis, AI can also assist in structuring evaluative writing. A student preparing a position paper or sermon can use AI to review argument flow, anticipate counterpoints, or test the clarity of their reasoning. These functions do not replace the need for critical thought but can help students become more aware of weaknesses or assumptions in their logic. Moreover, by interacting with AI-generated content that challenges their theological stance, students are pushed to defend their positions with greater clarity, humility, and depth, refining their ability to articulate and justify their convictions within a broader theological conversation.

Nevertheless, evaluation must always be framed within a larger ethos of theological formation. The goal is not simply to "win" an argument or critique for its own sake, but to arrive at a deeper understanding of God's truth and its implications for human flourishing. AI must not become a tool of polemics or overconfidence. Rather, it should be used to stretch students' thinking, cultivate intellectual humility, and foster the kind of wise, prayerful judgment that ministry requires. When supported by wise instruction and a formative learning community, AI-assisted evaluation can become a meaningful part of the theological learning process—shaping students into reflective practitioners who can think critically, lead faithfully, and discern with spiritual maturity.

## Creating: Generating Sermons, Theological Reflections, or Liturgies Using Prompts

The creative dimension of theological education is where students begin to synthesize what they've learned into new expressions of faith, proclamation, and pastoral practice. This level of higher-order thinking is deeply formational: it challenges students to construct sermons that preach the gospel with contextual sensitivity, write theological reflections that address pressing contemporary questions, and craft liturgies that invite communities into meaningful worship. Creation is not merely a display of academic competence or artistic flair; it is a theological act that invites students to embody their learning in ways that serve the Church, glorify God, and engage the world with truth and grace.

Artificial intelligence can serve as a valuable partner in this creative process, offering tools that stimulate imagination, support structure, and invite exploration. For example, a student might prompt an AI tool to generate different sermon outlines on the parable of the prodigal son, each emphasizing a different theological theme — grace, repentance, reconciliation, or the justice of God. These outlines provide starting points for the student to consider how a text might be preached to different audiences, helping them reflect on varying pastoral needs, cultural contexts, and theological emphases.

Likewise, AI can support the writing of prayers, calls to worship, and liturgical responses by offering models or adapting existing forms to fit themes or settings. A student designing a liturgy for Pentecost could use AI to explore various approaches to the day and then generate language that aligns with their community's ethos. In this way, AI can act as a dialogue partner — offering suggestions, presenting possibilities, and expanding the student's theological and spiritual vocabulary as they seek to express faith in ways that are both rooted and imaginative.

However, creation in theological education must be more than clever output — it must reflect the integration of Scripture, tradition, reason, and experience in ways that are personally owned and pastorally rooted. Students must be guided to move beyond AI-generated drafts into work that is authentically theirs, shaped by prayer, reflection, and deep theological wrestling. AI may offer helpful scaffolding, but it is the student who must construct the final offering — a sermon preached with conviction, a prayer formed through personal devotion, or a theological reflection shaped by deep engagement with Scripture and community.

When used wisely, AI can assist in fostering the creative dimension of theological formation, helping students take the risk of expression and move from passive receivers to active theologians. Yet, as always, the educator plays a critical role in ensuring that such creativity is not merely efficient, but faithful marked by theological depth, pastoral sensitivity, and spiritual integrity.

## Cautions: Distinguishing AI Generation from Student Authorship

As artificial intelligence becomes more integrated into the academic and ministerial work of theological students, it raises important questions about authorship, integrity, and formation. While AI can assist students in creative, analytical, and evaluative tasks, it must not obscure the distinction between supportive input and personal ownership. Theological education is not simply about producing content — it is about shaping persons. This means that the work students submit must ultimately reflect their own theological reasoning, spiritual discernment, and academic integrity, shaped through personal study, reflection, and engagement with their learning community.

Educators and institutions have a responsibility to establish clear guidelines that define what constitutes appropriate use of AI. These guidelines should not be overly punitive or fear-driven, but formative and transparent, helping students understand when and how AI tools can ethically be incorporated into their learning process. For instance, using AI to brainstorm sermon outlines or summarize a dense theological text may be acceptable if it is part of a process the student actively engages and discerns, contributing their own voice, interpretation, and theological insight along the way.

Transparency is key. Students should be encouraged to disclose their use of AI tools in the same way they might cite a source or acknowledge a conversation that shaped their thinking. This fosters an academic culture rooted in trust, where learning is valued not for its polish but for its authenticity. Moreover, reflection should be part of the learning process — asking students not just what they created, but how they arrived at it, and how any technological assistance informed their theological decisions, shaped their understanding, or challenged their assumptions.

Ultimately, the goal of theological education is not to replicate information but to form wise, discerning, faithful leaders who can think theologically in real-world situations. When students outsource their thinking or creativity entirely to AI, they short-circuit the very process of formation that theological study is intended to cultivate. The use of AI must therefore be guided by a commitment to integrity, spiritual growth, and academic responsibility. If framed with care, AI can be a valuable companion in the learning journey — serving not as a replacement for human thought or spiritual discernment, but as a tool that supports growth, fosters exploration, and enhances theological formation when used with integrity.

## Conclusion: Forming Theologically Reflective Leaders in the Age of AI

Theological education has always aimed higher than mere information transfer; it seeks the transformation of students into thoughtful, discerning, and faithful leaders of the Church. Higher-order thinking skills — applying, analyzing, evaluating, and creating — are not simply academic achievements; they are acts of theological responsibility. They shape how students preach, counsel, lead, and live as bearers of the gospel in a complex world. Artificial intelligence, when used wisely, can support this formative process by extending the reach of instruction, personalizing learning experiences, and providing new avenues for students to engage theological content with depth and creativity.

In each domain of higher-order thinking, AI offers tools that prompt students to think more deeply, engage more broadly, and express themselves more clearly. From simulated pastoral scenarios to comparative doctrinal analysis, from critical evaluation of arguments to creative expression in sermons and liturgy, AI can assist learners in refining their voice and strengthening their theological insight. But these benefits are only realized when technology serves a larger vision of formation — one that centers on the cultivation of wisdom, spiritual maturity, and a deep commitment to the Church's mission in the world.

As educators, we must guide students not only in how to use AI, but in how to think with wisdom, create with integrity, and evaluate with spiritual maturity. The future of theological education will be shaped not simply by which tools we use, but by how faithfully we form students to use them. In this sense, AI is not a threat to theological formation — it is a test of it. And when our pedagogy is rooted in the character of Christ, the wisdom of the tradition, and the power of the Spirit, it is a test we are well-prepared to meet — forming leaders who can navigate the challenges of technological change with faithfulness, clarity, and grace.

# Chapter 8
## Hybrid and Online Models Using AI

**Introduction**

    The landscape of theological education is shifting rapidly, shaped by the convergence of digital innovation, global accessibility needs, and evolving student expectations. Traditional residential models, while still valuable, are no longer the only — or even primary — modes of formation for many seminaries and divinity schools. Hybrid and online models now serve a growing number of learners who seek flexibility without sacrificing depth, community, or rigor. In this context, artificial intelligence emerges not as a replacement for the educator, but as a tool that can enhance access, personalize learning, and support formation across a variety of digital learning environments.

    AI's role in this evolving educational ecosystem is not simply about efficiency or convenience — it is about extending and enriching the formative mission of theological institutions. When thoughtfully integrated, AI can help educators reimagine pedagogical strategies, tailor content delivery to diverse learners, and foster dynamic engagement in digital spaces. It also opens new possibilities for spiritual formation and ministerial preparation in asynchronous, cross-cultural, and multimodal environments.

    This chapter explores how AI can support hybrid and online theological education through three core areas: flipped classrooms, HyFlex and asynchronous formats; integration within learning management systems (LMS); and the design of meaningful student engagement through digital collaboration, discussion, and mentorship. Rather than treating AI as a threat to traditional teaching, this chapter frames it as a companion in the sacred task of formation—one that, when guided by theological vision and pastoral discernment, can enhance the depth, accessibility, and relational integrity of theological education.

As theological education adapts to the realities of an increasingly digital world, institutions are turning to hybrid and online models to reach a broader, more diverse student population. While these models offer flexibility, accessibility, and innovation, they also raise significant pedagogical questions about presence, engagement, and formation. Artificial intelligence, when integrated thoughtfully, can enhance these models by personalizing instruction, enriching collaboration, and creating new venues for formative engagement that transcend the boundaries of time and space.

**Flipped Classrooms**

Flipped classrooms, HyFlex formats, and asynchronous learning each provide a unique structure for delivering theological education beyond the traditional, in-person classroom. Among these, the flipped classroom offers a particularly dynamic approach by reimagining how time is used both inside and outside of class. Instead of relying on lecture as the primary mode of in-person instruction, the flipped classroom invites students to engage with theological content—such as video lectures, assigned readings, or multimedia resources—before class, so that classroom time can be devoted to active learning through discussion, case studies, peer collaboration, and pastoral application.

Artificial intelligence significantly enhances the flipped classroom model by enriching both the pre-class and in-class learning experiences. Before class, AI tools can generate concise summaries of assigned readings, helping students grasp essential themes and arguments. Intelligent quiz generators can provide formative assessments that gauge comprehension in real time, allowing students to identify areas of confusion and come to class prepared with focused questions. These quizzes can be adaptive, adjusting their difficulty based on student responses, and providing targeted explanations that reinforce key theological concepts or clarify misunderstandings in real time.

Moreover, AI can assist instructors by analyzing student responses to pre-class content, highlighting trends in misunderstanding or interest, and equipping the educator to tailor in-class discussions accordingly. During class, AI-driven resources such as chat-based theological tutors or interactive scenario simulations can support students as they work through complex applications of doctrine, ethics, or biblical interpretation in groups. Rather than replacing the educator, these tools expand the capacity of instructors to foster deeper engagement, facilitate personalized learning, and respond more effectively to the diverse needs and questions of their students.

The flipped classroom, when integrated with AI, becomes a space not only of content delivery but of active theological construction. It supports the movement from passive reception to dialogical, interpretive, and ministerial practice. For theological education, this means greater potential to cultivate leaders who are not merely informed, but engaged —

who are learning to think critically, speak faithfully, and serve wisely in community.

## HyFlex (Hybrid-Flexible)

HyFlex (Hybrid-Flexible) models offer students the ability to participate in theological education through multiple modalities—attending in-person, joining synchronously online, or engaging asynchronously—based on their context, availability, and learning preferences. This format holds significant promise for seminaries and theological schools seeking to serve diverse, global student bodies, including bivocational pastors, international learners, and those with family or ministry constraints. HyFlex empowers students to choose how they engage each week—whether in person, live online, or through recorded and interactive content—without sacrificing access to community, instruction, or formative learning experiences.

Artificial intelligence plays a critical role in supporting the complexity of HyFlex environments. Because students are engaging with content and one another in different ways, AI can assist instructors in managing and bridging these modalities. For example, AI tools can automatically generate transcripts or summaries of live class sessions, making them accessible to asynchronous learners. AI can also help synthesize discussion threads from in-person and online forums, ensuring that all voices— regardless of their mode of participation—are recognized, connected, and woven into the broader learning community.

Instructors can also leverage AI-driven scheduling and content-recommendation features to offer personalized learning pathways. For instance, students who miss a live lecture might receive AI-curated materials that align with their learning history or performance, helping them stay on track without falling behind. These tools help maintain pedagogical consistency across formats while respecting the flexibility that HyFlex promises.

However, the use of AI in HyFlex environments must be accompanied by intentional design and pastoral awareness. It is not enough to ensure that content is accessible; the relational and formational dimensions of theological education must also be preserved. AI can support but not replace the educator's presence in each modality — whether through personal engagement in a Zoom breakout room, feedback on a forum post, or prayerful presence in a classroom. When guided by a vision for holistic formation, AI helps sustain the coherence, accessibility, and relational depth of HyFlex learning, ensuring that every student — no matter how they engage — is drawn into a meaningful process of theological reflection and spiritual growth.

## Asynchronous Learning

Asynchronous learning allows students to engage theological content on their own schedule, offering flexibility that is especially valuable for adult learners, international students, and those with significant ministry or family responsibilities. In this model, course materials — lectures, readings, assignments, and discussion forums — are made available through a learning platform, and students are given the freedom to interact with them within defined timeframes. While this mode can risk becoming isolating or overly transactional, it also holds immense potential for reflective, self-directed theological engagement when paired with intentional design and appropriate technological support.

Artificial intelligence can significantly enhance asynchronous learning by making content more interactive, adaptive, and responsive to each student's progress. For instance, AI can generate summaries or highlight key concepts from dense theological texts, allowing students to quickly grasp essential ideas before diving deeper. It can also provide automated feedback on assignments or discussion posts, encouraging students to refine their thinking and more actively engage with the material. These tools can provide real-time encouragement, clarification, or challenge, helping students remain intellectually engaged and spiritually attentive even in the absence of a live classroom environment.

Another advantage of AI in asynchronous learning lies in its capacity to monitor participation and engagement. By analyzing student activities such as reading patterns, quiz performance, or discussion contributions, AI can alert instructors when students might be struggling or disengaged. This allows educators to intervene with timely support, ensuring that asynchronous learning does not become passive or disconnected. Rather, it can be a rich, reflective space where students have time to process and internalize theological ideas, connect them to their lived experiences, and articulate their understanding with greater depth and clarity.

Perhaps most importantly, AI can help preserve the theological and formational depth of asynchronous learning by facilitating structured opportunities for reflection, spiritual integration, and community connection. For example, students might interact with an AI companion that poses weekly theological questions, invites them to reflect on ministry experiences, or suggests Scripture passages aligned with the week's theme. While this engagement is virtual, it can still be spiritually formative when shaped by thoughtful prompts, guided reflection, and integration with communal practices of worship, prayer, and dialogue.

When combined with thoughtful course design and pastoral presence, AI-enhanced asynchronous learning can offer more than just convenience — it can be a spiritually meaningful mode of theological education, one that respects the rhythms of students' lives while deepening their engagement with God, the Church, and the world.

## Learning Management Systems (LMS)

Learning Management Systems (LMS) form the digital infrastructure for most hybrid and online theological programs. Platforms such as Canvas, Moodle, or Blackboard organize content, manage communication, track grades, and support student progress. Integrating artificial intelligence into these systems adds a new layer of responsiveness, personalization, and instructional efficiency that can enrich the educational experience for both students and instructors.

AI can automate routine administrative tasks such as grading quizzes, flagging incomplete assignments, or sending reminders for due dates — freeing faculty to focus on mentorship and spiritual guidance. But beyond logistics, AI can act as an instructional partner within the LMS environment. For example, an AI assistant embedded in a course module might recommend supplemental readings based on a student's quiz performance or provide clarification when a student struggles with a theological concept. In this way, AI becomes more than a backend utility, it becomes a pedagogical presence that supports students learning in real time, adapting to their needs and reinforcing key concepts as they progress through the course.

Another key function of AI in LMS platforms is data analysis. By tracking patterns of engagement — such as how frequently students log in, where they spend the most time, or which resources they revisit — AI tools can help instructors identify at-risk students or adapt content delivery to better meet student needs. This kind of insight enables timely pastoral and academic support, ensuring that students don't fall through the cracks in a digital environment.

AI can also support formative assessment by offering personalized feedback on assignments, discussion posts, or reflections. Instead of receiving only end-of-course evaluations, students can receive in-the-moment insights that guide their theological reasoning and expression. This real-time feedback loop fosters deeper engagement and reinforces learning while it's happening, not just after the fact.

At its best, AI integration within LMS environments creates an educational space that is not only efficient but also formational. It allows for adaptive learning paths, individualized support, and more intentional faculty presence — even at scale. For theological education, this means that large or geographically dispersed classes can still experience rich engagement, responsive instruction, and personalized spiritual formation.

## Design Engagement: Discussion Boards, AI Companions, and Collaborative Work

One of the most pressing challenges in hybrid and online theological education is fostering meaningful engagement — both between students and with the material itself. Without the natural rhythms of in-person conversation or embodied communal practices, online learning can sometimes feel abstract or disconnected. Yet with thoughtful design and strategic use of AI, digital spaces can become sites of vibrant interaction, reflective dialogue, and collaborative theological formation.

AI can enhance traditional discussion boards by generating prompts that encourage deeper reflection, framing questions that draw connections between course content and lived experience, or offering summary insights from previous conversations to keep discussions cohesive. These intelligent prompts can help students move beyond surface-level responses, pushing them to wrestle with theological tensions, cite sources thoughtfully, and reflect theologically on ministry experiences. Additionally, AI can flag patterns of disengagement, repetition, or imbalance in student participation, allowing instructors to intervene with timely feedback or additional support to sustain meaningful dialogue.

AI companions—custom-designed chatbots or virtual tutors—can also serve as formative conversation partners. These tools can be programmed to simulate theological dialogue, ask guiding questions, or offer personalized feedback. For example, a student might engage with an AI companion that asks them to articulate the implications of a Christological doctrine for pastoral care, or to compare theological perspectives on a particular ethical issue. While these conversations are not a substitute for human face-to-face mentoring, they can serve as valuable supplements—extending the reach of instructors, encouraging theological curiosity, and offering students a safe space to explore ideas before bringing them into the broader learning community.

Collaborative work, which can be difficult to manage in asynchronous or hybrid formats, is also aided by AI tools that facilitate scheduling, communication, and workflow. AI can help create equitable group dynamics by tracking participation, identifying imbalances, or suggesting roles based on strengths and interests. It can also help synthesize shared contributions into draft outlines for group presentations or theological statements, streamlining the process without removing the need for critical human judgment, collaborative discernment, and theological reflection.

Ultimately, engagement is not just a pedagogical concern but a theological one. The formation of ministers, scholars, and leaders depends on shared reflection, mutual encouragement, and theological conversation. AI, when integrated with care, can support this engagement by creating relational bridges in digital spaces, scaffolding meaningful collaboration, and drawing students into deeper communion with one another and with the truth they are studying. The goal is not to automate conversation, but to cultivate spaces where genuine theological dialogue can flourish — spaces that are enriched, not replaced, by the thoughtful integration of AI.

## Conclusion: Designing for Presence, Formation, and Innovation

Theological education is being reshaped not only by necessity but by possibility. Hybrid and online learning models, once viewed as compromises to traditional formation, are now maturing into spaces of genuine academic and spiritual depth — especially when guided by intentional design and theological imagination. Artificial intelligence, when thoughtfully integrated, amplifies the strengths of these modalities. It enables flexibility without sacrificing rigor, fosters connection amid dispersion, and supports formation that is both intellectually rich and spiritually grounded.

As we have seen, AI can enrich flipped classrooms by supporting preparation and maximizing in-person engagement. It can strengthen HyFlex and asynchronous formats by ensuring pedagogical coherence and preserving spiritual presence across multiple learning environments. Through learning management systems and carefully designed engagement strategies, AI becomes a partner in cultivating reflection, conversation, and collaboration — hallmarks of theological formation.

Still, the aim is not technological sophistication for its own sake. The goal is to create learning environments that honor the human person, serve the mission of the Church, and cultivate wisdom for ministry in a rapidly changing world. Instructors and institutions must remain theologically anchored and pedagogically discerning, using AI not as a replacement for relational teaching but as an extension of it. When we place formation at the center and deploy AI as a servant to that end, we create the conditions for a learning environment where technology enhances, rather than eclipses, the sacred work of theological education.

# Chapter 9
## Theological Case Studies Using AI

**Introduction**

Theological education is not merely about transferring information — it is about forming ministers, scholars, and leaders who can think critically, act compassionately, and embody wisdom in the complexity of real life. Case-based learning has long served this goal by immersing students in scenarios that require discernment, integration of knowledge, and pastoral imagination. In the digital age, artificial intelligence introduces new possibilities for creating and engaging theological case studies that ask students to interpret, respond, and lead with theological depth, forming habits of pastoral wisdom and practical theology through embodied, scenario-based learning.

AI's ability to simulate nuanced situations, represent diverse voices, and process complex theological material makes it a natural partner in case-based pedagogy. No longer limited to static case descriptions, educators can now design dynamic, interactive experiences that respond to student choices, model historical events, or generate theological analogies with precision and depth. Across disciplines — from pastoral care to biblical exegesis — AI can offer tools that support deeper reflection, broaden perspectives across traditions and contexts, and foster the kind of theological imagination essential for faithful ministry today.

This chapter explores how AI can be used to generate and support theological case studies in four primary areas: practical theology, church history, systematic theology, and biblical studies. Through specific applications and pedagogical strategies, we will consider not only the technical possibilities but the spiritual and ethical implications of using AI to train students in theological discernment. At stake is not simply efficiency or innovation, but the formation of leaders equipped to serve the Church with faithfulness and insight, prepared not only to think critically but to minister compassionately in a world shaped by rapid technological and cultural change.

## Reimagining Case-Based Learning Through Artificial Intelligence

As theological education continues to evolve in the digital age, case-based learning remains one of the most effective pedagogical tools for bridging the gap between abstract doctrine and embodied ministry. Case studies situate theological reflection within the lived complexity of human experience. They require students to integrate biblical interpretation, historical insight, doctrinal clarity, and pastoral wisdom—moving beyond theoretical knowledge toward contextual discernment and practical faithfulness that prepares them for the real complexities of ministry.

Artificial intelligence offers an unprecedented opportunity to revitalize and reimagine case-based learning for this new era. No longer confined to printed case scenarios or static discussion prompts, instructors can now generate dynamic, context-sensitive, and interactive case studies that evolve in response to student input. AI can simulate realistic pastoral conversations, create fictional congregational profiles, or generate morally complex dilemmas that challenge students to wrestle with Scripture, theology, and ethics in real time, while receiving formative feedback and support.

The real gift of AI in this context is not merely efficiency or novelty, but theological depth and pedagogical possibility. With the right guidance, AI-generated case studies can reflect the diversity of the global Church, incorporate perspectives from various traditions, and explore ministry challenges in urban, rural, multicultural, or digitally networked environments. This kind of engagement prepares students not just to know theology, but to live it — to think critically, act compassionately, and serve with conviction in diverse and demanding ministry contexts where clear answers are rare, but faithful presence is essential.

By integrating AI into case-based theological education, we do not remove the human element — we elevate it. Educators are empowered to focus on mentorship and theological guidance, while students are invited into immersive experiences that sharpen their judgment, refine their spiritual instincts, and deepen their formation. In this reimagined space, theological education becomes not only more engaging, but more faithful to the real-world demands of ministry in a rapidly changing world where adaptability, wisdom, and deeply rooted formation are indispensable.

## Practical Theology: Simulating Ministry Through AI-Driven Case Studies

In the realm of practical theology, artificial intelligence can become a powerful tool for preparing students to meet the demands of real-life ministry. By generating realistic case studies in pastoral care, congregational leadership, and ethical decision-making, AI offers students the opportunity to practice wisdom and theological reflection in lifelike scenarios. These AI-generated situations can mirror the kinds of pastoral complexities that arise every day — navigating grief after the death of a child, addressing marital conflict, responding to mental health crises, or guiding congregants through ethical tensions involving work, family, or social justice.

Unlike static textbook examples, AI-driven case studies can unfold in real time, allowing students to respond conversationally to digital characters who express emotion, confusion, or spiritual need. These characters may come from diverse cultural backgrounds, theological perspectives, or life situations, helping students develop sensitivity to difference and contextual nuance. Through these interactions, learners are encouraged to apply pastoral theology in responsive, compassionate, and discerning ways, learning to navigate conversations that require emotional intelligence, theological integrity, and a pastoral heart attuned to the needs of the other.

Moreover, ethical decision-making scenarios generated by AI can help students engage moral complexity with theological rigor. Whether confronting a congregant's disclosure of abuse, considering the ethics of wealth distribution in a church budget, or navigating a conflict between denominational policy and pastoral care, students can be challenged to reason through competing values, scriptural imperatives, and ecclesial norms. AI can simulate multiple outcomes based on student decisions, fostering reflection on the theological and pastoral implications of each choice, while also encouraging students to examine how their own biases, assumptions, and formation shape their decision-making processes.

AI also supports formative feedback by offering students immediate insights into their theological reasoning, emotional intelligence, and decision-making patterns. It can suggest Scripture passages, theological frameworks, or historical examples that might inform a more robust pastoral response. Though not a substitute for faculty mentorship or peer discussion, AI can scaffold learning in ways that build student confidence and deepen spiritual discernment, helping them integrate classroom learning with the pastoral judgment required for ministry in complex, real-world contexts.

Ultimately, the integration of AI into practical theology case studies allows students to rehearse the sacred art of ministry in a low risk but deeply formative environment. These digital simulations, when framed within a strong theological pedagogy, prepare students to enter real pastoral situations not only with theoretical knowledge, but with practiced wisdom, compassionate presence, and a heart attuned to the Spirit's guidance, so that when they encounter real people in moments of pain, crisis, or moral conflict, they do so as wise and faithful shepherds rather than inexperienced technicians.

## Church History: Immersive Encounters with the Past through AI Simulation

Church history education is also enriched through AI-generated case studies that invite students not just to study the past, but to inhabit it. Through advanced language modeling and contextual training, AI can simulate dialogues with historical figures, enabling students to step into pivotal theological moments with a sense of immediacy and interaction. Rather than simply reading about Augustine's debates with Pelagius or the theological tensions at the Council of Nicaea, students can experience these events as participants — interacting with key figures, testing arguments, and grasping the stakes of doctrinal development in real time.

These simulations allow students to pose questions to AI-generated figures who respond in historically grounded voices. For example, an AI rendering of Martin Luther might offer insights on justification shaped by his writings, while a simulated conversation with Julian of Norwich could introduce students to mystical theology from within a medieval worldview. The purpose is not to romanticize the past but to engage it—to hear historical voices in context, appreciate theological development over time, and reflect on how inherited traditions continue to shape the Church's witness in the present age.

Instructors can also use AI to build case studies that place students within historical crises—such as the decision-making of church leaders during the Reformation, the challenges of Christianity under empire, or the theological struggles of Christians facing modernity. These reconstructed moments ask students to consider what theological, ethical, and pastoral decisions were made, why they mattered, and how they might respond in similar circumstances. Such immersive learning cultivates historical empathy and theological discernment, challenging students to consider not only what happened, but what was at stake for the Church's identity, mission, and faithfulness amid social and theological upheaval.

Importantly, these AI-generated reenactments must be used with discernment. While they offer innovative pathways into church history, they also require careful framing to avoid flattening theological nuance or oversimplifying complex contexts. When guided well, however, these tools can draw students into rich, dialogical engagement with the cloud of witnesses who have shaped Christian faith across centuries, helping them recognize continuity and discontinuity in the Church's ongoing theological journey.

AI becomes not a replacement for primary source analysis or historical scholarship, but a dynamic supplement that helps students grasp the living tradition of the Church. By making historical theology interactive, AI allows learners to see the past not as a distant archive, but as a source of wisdom, conversation, and discernment for the challenges of today 's Church and its future leaders.

## Systematic Theology: Structuring Complexity with AI Support

Systematic theology challenges students to explore the coherence and interrelation of doctrinal claims about God, humanity, salvation, the Church, and eschatology. It asks them to trace the logic of the Christian faith, synthesize vast theological traditions, and articulate a faithful, ordered account of belief. Yet for many learners, the abstract nature of systematic theology can be intimidating. AI offers a set of tools that can help students navigate this complexity, not by simplifying theology, but by helping them visualize, compare, and articulate its underlying coherence in intellectually and spiritually meaningful ways.

AI can assist students in generating analogies that bring difficult doctrines to life — illuminating the mystery of the Trinity, for example, with imagery drawn from music, art, or relational dynamics. These analogies, when crafted thoughtfully, become entry points for deeper understanding and conversation. AI can also suggest cross-traditional comparisons, such as contrasting Calvinist and Arminian perspectives on election, or exploring sacramental theology in Catholic, Orthodox, and Reformed contexts. This approach encourages theological hospitality and critical engagement, as students learn to appreciate the internal logic of differing traditions and refine their own convictions through informed comparison and creative reflection.

Diagramming tools enhanced by AI can visually map out the structure of theological systems, highlighting how one belief informs or depends upon another. For example, students might create a visual theology of salvation that connects doctrines of sin, grace, justification, and sanctification across historical traditions. These diagrams can serve as springboards for discussion, critique, and constructive theological development. AI can help identify where a student's system lacks internal coherence or where theological assumptions may need clarification, ultimately supporting the construction of more rigorous, integrated, and faithful expressions of belief.

Additionally, AI can facilitate intertextual theological exploration — drawing connections between theological claims and their biblical, historical, and philosophical sources. A student researching the nature of Christ's atonement might receive a synthesis of relevant patristic commentary, Reformation insights, and 20th-century responses. This kind of comparative mapping does not remove the burden of research but enhances it by offering pathways into deeper inquiry and theological synthesis, encouraging students to engage tradition not as a static inheritance but as a living conversation.

Ultimately, AI serves not as a doctrinal authority, but as a tutor in theological reasoning. When used within a framework of accountability and formation, these tools can help students develop clarity, humility, and creativity in articulating their theological convictions. The work of systematic theology remains profoundly human and spiritual — but with AI as a thoughtful assistant, students can explore the breadth of Christian thought with greater structure, insight, and depth, cultivating the skills of theologians who are both precise and pastoral.

## Biblical Studies: Enhancing Exegesis and Interpretation with AI

Biblical studies, rooted in the careful interpretation of Scripture, demands rigorous attention to language, context, history, and theological meaning. Students must learn not only how to read the biblical text closely, but how to situate it within its literary, canonical, and theological frameworks. Artificial intelligence offers emerging tools that can support this task—not by interpreting Scripture on behalf of the student, but by offering aids to understanding that deepen engagement with the sacred text and cultivating disciplined, reverent study.

AI-driven tools can assist in interlinear analysis, helping students study the original Hebrew and Greek texts with greater ease. These tools can identify key grammatical structures, parse difficult verb forms, and visually display word relationships across translations. Instead of replacing the need to study biblical languages, such tools can reinforce learning by giving students immediate feedback and visual reinforcement, helping them internalize the grammar, vocabulary, and syntax of Scripture in its original form.

In addition, AI can support exegetical work by offering outlines of passage structure, identifying rhetorical devices, and highlighting intertextual connections across the biblical canon. For example, when working with a text from Isaiah, AI might surface allusions in the Gospels, suggest structural parallels in the Psalms, or highlight thematic echoes in Revelation. This helps students trace the unity and diversity of

Scripture and recognize how theological themes unfold across time and genre, fostering a more holistic and canonical approach to biblical theology.

AI tools can also play a constructive role in sermon preparation. Based on a selected passage and a particular context—such as preaching to a grieving congregation, addressing social injustice, or guiding seasonal liturgy—AI can offer outlines, illustration ideas, or theological questions that prompt deeper reflection. Used well, these resources do not supply ready-made sermons but rather encourage students to think critically, pastorally, and theologically about their audience and their interpretive responsibility, cultivating sermons that are both biblically grounded and contextually faithful.

When integrated with discernment and guided by sound hermeneutical principles, AI can serve as a companion to the sacred task of interpreting Scripture. It aids in illuminating the richness of the text, while keeping students grounded in the interpretive responsibility that comes with handling the Word of God. The goal is not speed or automation, but depth, reverence, and the formation of interpreters who are both faithful to the text and attentive to the needs of the community they serve.

## Conclusion

Theological education is ultimately about formation—shaping students not only in what they know, but in how they think, act, pray, and lead. Case-based learning has long served this purpose by immersing students in complex, lifelike scenarios that require discernment, theological reflection, and pastoral imagination. By blending centuries-old pedagogical methods with cutting-edge AI capabilities, theological education can cultivate deeper insight, foster integrative thinking, and better prepare students for the diverse realities of ministry today.

Used wisely, AI does not distance students from lived theology—it draws them deeper into it. It offers safe but meaningful spaces to practice pastoral responses, to wrestle with ethical dilemmas, to encounter voices from the Church's past, and to organize complex theological systems into coherent thought. The goal is not technological novelty, but human and spiritual maturity: helping students become leaders who can navigate ambiguity, exercise theological judgment, and serve communities with wisdom and compassion grounded in the gospel.

As educators, we must shape these tools with discernment. AI must never become a substitute for prayerful engagement, relational learning, or the guiding presence of the Holy Spirit. But when integrated into a theologically grounded pedagogy, AI-generated case studies can be a profound asset—awakening imagination, reinforcing formation, and preparing students to think and minister with faithfulness and courage in an increasingly complex world where clarity and presence are most needed.

# Chapter 10
## Capstone Projects and AI Collaboration

**Introduction**

Capstone projects serve as the culmination of a student's theological education, offering a space where academic inquiry, spiritual formation, and ministerial imagination converge. In these final expressions of learning—whether research-based, praxis-oriented, or creative—students are called to integrate their studies into a coherent and meaningful offering to the Church and academy. As theological education enters an era of digital transformation, artificial intelligence presents both new possibilities and necessary questions. How can AI be used in ways that support student learning without diminishing intellectual integrity or spiritual depth? How might it assist in the creative and formative work that capstones demand? This chapter explores the role of AI in designing, supporting, and guiding capstone projects, always with an eye toward sustaining the theological virtues of originality, discernment, and faithful authorship.

**Designing Theological Capstones in the Age of AI**

Capstone projects mark a pivotal moment in graduate theological education—a culmination of intellectual growth, spiritual formation, and ministerial preparation. Whether in the form of a thesis, final paper, sermon series, creative project, or ministry portfolio, these summative assessments call students to integrate what they have learned across biblical studies, theology, history, ethics, and pastoral practice. In this context, artificial intelligence can serve as a dynamic companion to both student and educator, enriching the capstone experience while preserving the essential virtues of creativity, discernment, and faithful authorship.

Designing capstone experiences in a digital age invites educators to imagine new forms of synthesis and evaluation. Rather than simply assessing mastery of content, capstones can become spaces for generative theological workspaces where students not only demonstrate knowledge but create something meaningful for the Church and world. AI can assist in shaping these summative assessments by helping generate project prompts, simulate ministry contexts, or provide scaffolding for interdisciplinary connections. For instance, a capstone in practical theology might be designed around a pastoral care intervention informed by biblical exegesis, systematic reflection, and community engagement, with AI modeling congregational profiles or offering research leads on relevant social issues. The educator's role remains central: guiding the formation of the project, providing accountability, and ensuring that technological tools serve the theological task, not define it.

## AI as Research Assistant: Supporting Without Replacing Authorship

Throughout the capstone journey, AI can serve as a versatile assistant—helping students gather resources, clarify ideas, and refine drafts. As a research assistant, AI can suggest bibliographies, provide brief summaries of theological works, or direct students toward lesser-known sources. This can be especially helpful for students unfamiliar with navigating theological databases or complex academic texts. As a tutor, AI can prompt students with guiding questions that stimulate deeper reflection, offer counterarguments that strengthen analytical skills, and organize outlines for clearer structure. In the editorial phase, AI can identify inconsistencies in argumentation, suggest improvements in clarity and flow, and assist with grammar and formatting. Despite these useful features, however, the student must retain intellectual and spiritual ownership of their work. Theological reasoning, interpretive nuance, and pastoral imagination cannot be automated. A capstone project should not merely be a polished paper; it must be an authentic expression of the student's formation and theological voice. The role of AI is to aid, not to author. Faculty must cultivate a culture of academic integrity and reflective use of AI, ensuring students understand both the benefits and the ethical boundaries of technological assistance.

## Creativity and Discernment: Forming Theological Voice in a Digital Age

Capstone projects are not merely academic exercises—they are occasions for students to synthesize their formation and express their theological imagination in ways that are intellectually rigorous and spiritually meaningful. AI can support this process by sparking creativity and offering pathways into new forms of theological articulation. For instance, a student might use generative AI to draft a liturgical poem, storyboard a multimedia sermon series, or explore cross-cultural theological metaphors. These tools can help students break through writer's block or visualize abstract concepts in new ways. However, creativity in theological education must be guided by discernment. The goal is not novelty for its own sake, but faithful innovation rooted in Scripture, tradition, and the needs of the community. AI should never short-circuit the process of wrestling with hard questions or bypass the struggle to speak with one's own voice. Instead, it should function as a supportive presence—stimulating ideas, offering structure, and helping students refine their expression. Faculty must help students reflect on how, why, and when they use AI in their creative process, cultivating not just technical skill but moral and theological responsibility.

## Capstones as Vocational Markers: Integrating Formation with Innovation

A well-designed capstone is more than an academic achievement; it is a vocational statement. It represents a student's readiness to lead, teach, preach, or serve in complex, real-world contexts. Integrating AI into the capstone process can equip students with relevant digital competencies while still honoring the deeply spiritual nature of their calling. When used wisely, AI allows students to engage broader sources, articulate ideas more clearly, and develop innovative forms of ministry or scholarship. These projects then become markers not only of academic progress but of vocational clarity—evidence that the student has wrestled with theological questions, listened to the Spirit, and discerned how to serve the Church in a digital age. But the success of such integration depends on how AI is framed within the theological curriculum. It must not be seen as a shortcut, but as a partner in disciplined inquiry and creative ministry. When students are formed to see AI not as a substitute for human insight but as a tool within a Spirit-guided process, capstones become spaces where tradition and innovation meet. They reflect not just what students know, but who they are becoming—and how they are being sent into the world to bear faithful witness.

## Conclusion

Capstone projects occupy a sacred place in the life of theological education. They are more than academic assessments; they are moments of integration, discernment, and calling. As artificial intelligence becomes an increasingly present reality in both educational and ministerial contexts, theological institutions must learn to embrace it with wisdom, clarity, and conviction. When used thoughtfully, AI can enhance capstone experiences — serving as a research assistant, creative partner, and structural support — without compromising the spiritual and intellectual integrity of the student's work.

Yet the heart of the capstone must remain untouched by automation. These projects must reflect the student's own theological journey, shaped by years of study, prayer, community, and pastoral vision. AI may help students express what they've learned, but it cannot supply what they alone must bring: the voice forged through struggle, the insight borne of faith, and the clarity that emerges from sustained reflection.

Ultimately, capstone projects serve not only as endings but as thresholds. They point beyond themselves to the ministries, writings, and witnesses each student will offer to the world. By integrating AI as a supportive presence — rather than a controlling force — educators can help students enter that threshold with confidence, imagination, and a deep awareness of their vocation. In doing so, the Church is strengthened, the academy is renewed, and the next generation of theological leaders is prepared to engage a world in need of truth, beauty, and grace.

# Chapter 11
## The Risks and Dangers of AI in Theological Education

**Introduction**

As artificial intelligence becomes more deeply integrated into theological education, its promise is often greeted with enthusiasm. AI offers speed, efficiency, and support—qualities that can enhance learning and formation in powerful ways. Yet, as with any powerful tool, its benefits come with dangers. In a discipline rooted in deep reflection, personal transformation, and communal discernment, the risks posed by uncritical use of AI are substantial. If left unchecked, these risks threaten to erode not only the quality of theological scholarship but also the character of those entrusted to minister the Word of God. This chapter explores the key dangers AI presents to theological education and proposes pathways toward its responsible and redemptive use.

**Plagiarism, Over-Reliance, and Epistemic Laziness**

Among the most pressing concerns raised by AI in theological education is the threat of academic dishonesty—particularly plagiarism. The emergence of generative AI has blurred the lines between assistance and authorship. With just a few well-phrased prompts, students can generate essays, discussion responses, sermon outlines, or theological arguments that appear polished and original, yet originate not from their own thought, prayer, or study, but from an algorithm trained on massive datasets. The temptation to copy, modify, and submit such content as one's own undermines not only the integrity of academic work but the very character formation that theological education seeks to cultivate. Plagiarism is not simply a violation of policy; it is a breach of trust and vocation inherent to ministry preparation.

Beyond outright dishonesty, however, lies a more subtle and insidious danger: the gradual cultivation of over-reliance. When students grow accustomed to turning to AI tools for immediate answers, quick summaries, or theological synthesis, they risk developing shallow intellectual habits. The hard work of research, slow reading, contemplation, and wrestling with Scripture or theological texts can begin to feel unnecessary. Over time, this dependency on automation fosters what philosophers call "epistemic laziness"—a weakening of the will and desire to truly know. Instead of being formed as theologians and pastors who can discern, interpret, and communicate with depth and clarity, students may settle for the convenience of outsourced reasoning.

This laziness also affects the formation of theological imagination. Instead of prayerfully developing insight, drawing on lived experience, or engaging historical and ecclesial perspectives, students may receive pre-processed material that bypasses the very tensions that lead to wisdom. Theological education is not simply about acquiring information but about forming a heart and mind capable of engaging complexity with patience, humility, and hope. When AI tools become the primary avenue for engagement, students lose not only the depth of knowledge but also the sanctifying discomfort that comes with theological labor.

Moreover, the danger of epistemic laziness has implications beyond the classroom. If future pastors and leaders become habituated to asking AI for sermon illustrations, ethical positions, or biblical interpretations, they may fail to develop the pastoral instincts and theological grounding needed in real-life ministry. Machines can generate content, but they cannot discern hearts, read a room, or listen to the Spirit's movement in a congregation. A reliance on AI in formation risks producing leaders who are efficient but shallow—capable of managing data but not shepherding souls.

Addressing these risks requires vigilance from educators and institutions. It is not enough to warn against cheating; students must be formed to love the process of theological discovery. This includes cultivating intellectual virtues such as curiosity, perseverance, and reverence for truth. Faculty can design assessments that prioritize process over product, encourage collaborative interpretation, and require theological reflection that cannot be easily reproduced by machines. When theological education invites students into a community of inquiry shaped by grace and accountability, the temptations of plagiarism and laziness can be resisted not just by rule but by conviction.

## Theological Shallowness and the Loss of Community

One of the subtler yet most significant dangers of AI in theological education is the erosion of theological depth. AI systems excel at mimicking coherence and offering rapid responses to queries, but they do so without any sense of mystery, prayer, or spiritual discernment. While they can aggregate information and produce content that reads as logical or even insightful, they lack the capacity for theological wisdom—the slow, Spirit-led insight that arises from wrestling with God, tradition, Scripture, and community. As such, when AI becomes a student's primary partner in reflection, there is a real danger of mistaking surface-level synthesis for deep theological engagement.

This problem is particularly acute in a field like theology, which deals with ultimate concerns—God, human purpose, suffering, salvation, and justice. These are not merely academic questions; they are questions that require lived experience, community formation, and sustained contemplation. AI tools cannot pray, worship, suffer, or love. They cannot reflect on the mystery of the Trinity from a place of awe, nor can they discern the pastoral implications of a doctrinal belief within the life of a hurting congregation. When students rely too heavily on AI to draft theological responses, prepare sermons, or even generate prayerful reflections, they risk cultivating a theologically shallow imagination—one that is informationally rich but spiritually impoverished.

Alongside this shallowness comes the loss of community. Theological formation is inherently relational. It takes place not in isolation but through dialogue, disagreement, mentoring, and shared reflection. Class discussions, communal worship, hallway conversations, and late-night debates are not peripheral to theological education—they are essential. They embody the reality that truth is discovered in the community, not in a vacuum. But AI, for all its interactive sophistication, is not a community. It does not challenge, comfort, question, or laugh. It does not bear witness to faith in suffering or model embodied discipleship. As students increasingly turn to AI instead of one another or their professors, they miss the formative power of being shaped by and shaping—a community of learners.

This drift toward isolation is not only academic; it is pastoral. The ministry into which students are being formed is also fundamentally relational. Pastors, chaplains, and Christian leaders are called to walk alongside people, to be present in pain and celebration, to lead with wisdom grounded in communion. If formation occurs apart from community, there is a real risk that ministry will as well. Leaders formed in isolation may replicate that isolation in the congregations they serve, leaning on tools and technologies instead of flesh-and-blood relationships.

Therefore, theological institutions must be vigilant in fostering learning environments that privilege human connection, spiritual depth, and mutual accountability. This means designing assignments that require collaboration, creating space for embodied worship and shared discernment, and reminding students that theology is a communal task. It also means resisting the allure of AI-generated efficiency when it comes at the cost of communion. True theological depth is not produced by algorithms; it is cultivated in the crucible of community, through time, struggle, and grace.

## Guidelines for Responsible AI Use in Seminaries

While artificial intelligence presents numerous challenges to theological education, it also offers unique opportunities when approached with intentionality and discernment. Rather than simply prohibiting or uncritically embracing AI, seminaries are called to cultivate a culture of responsible, theologically grounded use — one that prioritizes formation over convenience and wisdom over speed. The development of clear guidelines for AI use is therefore an essential task for theological institutions seeking to navigate this new terrain faithfully.

First and foremost, seminaries must articulate an institutional vision for technology that aligns with their theological commitments. This vision should not be reactive, based solely on fears of misuse, but proactive, grounded in a positive theology of learning, human dignity, and spiritual formation. Policies surrounding AI use should grow out of this foundation, affirming that technology must always serve the purpose of forming wise, humble, and compassionate leaders for the Church and the world. These policies should address what kinds of AI use are permissible in various academic settings, distinguishing between appropriate assistance—such as brainstorming ideas or refining structure—and inappropriate use, such as generating entire assignments or circumventing the learning process.

Transparency is another key component. Students must be taught to disclose when and how AI tools were used in their work. This is not simply about academic honesty; it is about cultivating a habit of reflective engagement. If a student uses AI to organize a sermon outline or summarize a theological article, they should be encouraged to include a short reflection on what the tool offered and what interpretive work they contributed themselves. Such practices not only ensure accountability but also reinforce the importance of maintaining theological voice and agency.

Faculty members also bear responsibility in modeling responsible AI use. Professors should demonstrate how AI might serve as a conversation partner rather than a substitute for thought. Instructors can design assignments that require student process notes, peer engagement, or multi-stage submissions that cannot be easily generated in one pass. More importantly, they can foster classroom cultures that value deep inquiry, contemplation, and spiritual formation—cultures where students are formed to see technology not as a crutch, but as a tool that must be wielded wisely.

In addition, theological educators should intentionally incorporate conversations about AI into the curriculum itself. Courses in ethics, pastoral theology, and theological method can provide space for students to explore the theological implications of artificial intelligence. What does it mean to be human in an age of intelligent machines? How do we discern the difference between knowledge and wisdom, information and revelation? How might the Church engage a culture increasingly shaped by algorithmic logic? By raising these questions explicitly, seminaries prepare students to not only use AI responsibly in their studies but also to lead congregations and institutions in thinking critically about its place in the broader culture.

Finally, responsible AI use must be embedded in practices of community and spiritual discernment. Students should be encouraged to talk with mentors, peers, and spiritual directors about their use of technology in theological work. Faculty should pray with and for their students as they discern how best to engage these tools. Technological decisions should not be made in isolation but consider the Church's witness and the Spirit's leading. When theological education grounds its approach to AI in shared reflection, spiritual wisdom, and the character of Christ, it is possible to use this powerful tool without losing sight of the human and divine dimensions of formation.

## Conclusion

Artificial intelligence is here to stay, and theological education must respond not with fear, but with wisdom. The risks of plagiarism, intellectual laziness, theological superficiality, and communal isolation are significant, but they are not insurmountable. By naming these dangers and responding with clarity, accountability, and theological depth, seminaries can ensure that AI serves the formation of wise, faithful, and reflective leaders for the Church. Ultimately, the question is not whether AI will be used in theological education, but how — and whether its use will help students grow in the likeness of Christ or merely in the likeness of machines. Theological education must choose the former, for the sake of the gospel and the witness of the Church in a digitally saturated world.

# Chapter 12
## Spiritual and Formational Concerns

### Introduction

As theological education engages the possibilities and perils of artificial intelligence, one of the most pressing questions remains: Can technology form souls? While AI can assist with research, automate feedback, and generate content, spiritual formation requires something deeper, incarnational, relational, and mysterious. Theological education is not merely a transfer of information; it is a journey of transformation. This journey cannot be mechanized. It is rooted in prayer, shaped through community, and refined in the crucible of lived experience. As seminaries adopt digital tools and AI-enhanced learning environments, they must ensure that their commitment to spiritual and formational integrity remains central. This chapter explores the boundaries and possibilities of spiritual formation in the age of AI, offering theological insight and pedagogical vision.

### Can AI Shape Souls? The Role of Mentorship and Embodied Wisdom

At the heart of theological education lies a question that AI cannot answer with certainty, no matter how sophisticated its programming: Can souls be formed by machines? The answer, for many educators and spiritual leaders, is a clear and theologically grounded no. AI may aid cognition, enhance efficiency, or simulate conversation — but it cannot shape souls. Soul formation is a divine and relational process that happens over time, in the crucible of community, and under the guidance of the Holy Spirit. It involves not just the mind, but affection, imagination, conscience, and will. AI, for all its remarkable abilities, lacks a soul of its own — and therefore cannot shepherd one.

What shapes a soul is presence — presence to God, to oneself, to sacred texts, and to others in community. Mentorship in theological education embodies this presence. Whether in formal advising relationships or informal conversations over coffee, the wisdom that flows from seasoned guides is shaped by lived experience, spiritual maturity, and deep commitment to the formation of others. Mentors model patience, humility, and reverence for mystery. They ask difficult questions, listen with compassion, pray alongside their students, and offer guidance rooted not in abstraction but in embodied, storied faith. AI, even when it mimics human conversation or responds with stylistic theological fluency, cannot replicate this incarnational reality.

Moreover, mentorship is not transactional. It is covenantal. It grows through shared time, trust, and mutual vulnerability. A mentor can discern a student's gifts and fears. They can detect when a student is spiritually dry, when they are burdened by ministry fatigue, or when they are awakening to a deeper sense of call. These are not conditions that a machine can diagnose or address. They require prayerful attentiveness, pastoral intuition, and a relationship that respects the mystery of God's work in a human life. For this reason, seminary communities must guard and elevate embodied mentorship as a sacred trust — not just a pedagogical method but a form of spiritual accompaniment.

This has implications for how AI is used in theological settings. Tools that reduce theological education to a data-driven process—efficient but impersonal—risk short-circuiting the most vital part of formation: becoming more fully human in Christ. Soul formation cannot be accelerated. It cannot be scripted or automated. It emerges through faithful struggle, shared worship, lived ministry, and honest reflection. Mentorship invites students into that long obedience in the same direction. AI can supplement, but never substitute, this process.

In a time when many students are increasingly formed by digital culture—algorithmic thinking, instant answers, and curated identities—the seminary has a prophetic role to play. It must create space for slowness, silence, and relationships. It must elevate mentors not as experts dispensing content, but as wise guides cultivating souls. And it must remind students that their calling is not merely to produce sermons, papers, or strategies, but to become people whose very lives bear witness to the gospel. In that task, no machine can replace the sacred gift of human presence.

## Spiritual Disciplines and AI: Fostering Attention and Contemplation

Spiritual disciplines are the time-tested practices that train the soul to become attentive to God. In a theological context, they form the inner scaffolding that supports learning, discernment, and character development. Practices like silence, prayer, lectio divina, Sabbath, fasting, and examen are not add-ons to the academic journey; they are integral to the formation of ministers, theologians, and Christian leaders. These disciplines cultivate not only intellectual receptivity but the kind of spiritual depth necessary for navigating the mysteries of God and the complexities of human life. Yet these practices stand in stark contrast to the habits reinforced by artificial intelligence.

AI is built for speed, efficiency, and immediacy. It thrives on frictionless access to content and the automation of tasks. These strengths, when used without discernment, can subtly deform our attention — training us to skim rather than dwell, to consume rather than contemplate, to seek answers instead of sitting with questions. For theological students, who are called to dwell in mystery and live with theological tension, such habits can undermine the slow, sacred work of formation. Spiritual disciplines, by contrast, invite us into rhythms of receptivity, patience, and unhurried presence — qualities that are essential for deep theological reflection.

The challenge, then, is not simply whether AI can help with spiritual disciplines, but whether students and educators will create space for such disciplines in the first place. Can prayer be rushed through a prompt? Can discernment be outsourced to a chatbot? Can silence be scheduled between app notifications? These are not theoretical questions, they are lived ones. And they must be met with a pedagogical framework that prioritizes spiritual attention over digital acceleration.

That said, there are thoughtful ways to integrate AI without displacing the heart of formation. AI tools can generate Scripture reading plans, create reminders for daily prayer, or offer reflective questions that help students structure their time with God. But these tools must remain scaffolding, not substitutes. The goal is not more content but deeper communion. If AI is to support spiritual practice, it must do so in a way that protects the sacredness of encounter and resists the commodification of devotion.

Educators can help by modeling the importance of these practices within the structure of their courses. Creating space at the beginning of class for prayerful silence, inviting students to engage theological texts through lectio divina, or requiring personal reflection journals can help root academic work in spiritual attentiveness. These practices, when paired with careful engagement with AI tools, help students resist the numbing effect of speed and rediscover the beauty of stillness.

In an age of digital saturation, spiritual disciplines are countercultural acts. They remind us that formation is not found in the scroll, the swipe, or the search bar — but in the quiet voice of God, who speaks to those who make time to listen. AI may offer tools that support our rhythms, but it is the presence of God, not the presence of technology, that transforms the heart.

## Tech-Savvy Yet Soul-Rich Pedagogy

Theological educators today face the challenge — and opportunity — of cultivating a pedagogy that is both digitally informed and spiritually rooted. As AI and other emerging technologies become more deeply embedded in academic and ecclesial life, there is a growing need for instructional practices that are not only tech-savvy but also soul-rich. This balance is not easy to strike. Many institutions rush to adopt new technologies in the name of innovation, but in doing so risk abandoning the deeper goals of spiritual formation, character development, and vocational clarity. A truly faithful pedagogy must be formed by more than functionality; it must be governed by theological vision.

A tech-savvy pedagogy recognizes the realities of the digital world in which students live, work, and minister. It embraces the utility of AI for research assistance, writing refinement, content creation, and adaptive learning. It integrates learning management systems, collaborative tools, and digital platforms in ways that increase access and engagement. It helps students become literate in the technological tools they will encounter in ministry — from chatbots for pastoral triage to AI-driven analytics for church outreach. These are not trivial skills. They are necessary competencies for leaders who must navigate increasingly complex digital landscapes.

Yet a soul-rich pedagogy insists that these tools must serve, not supplant, the deeper aims of theological education. It prioritizes personal reflection over automated response, dialogue over data, formation over mere performance. Soul-rich learning happens in the sacred spaces of mentoring, worship, vulnerability, and community discernment. It asks not only what students know, but who they are becoming. It seeks to form students who are contemplative in their thinking, courageous in their leadership, and compassionate in their service — traits that no algorithm can teach.

Such a pedagogy also teaches discernment in the use of AI. Students are invited to consider not only how to use digital tools, but whether and when they should. They are encouraged to ask theological questions about technology: What vision of the human person does this tool assume? How does it shape my desires, my time, or my imagination? What does it enable me to see — or obscure? These questions form the crucible of ethical and spiritual maturity in a world where the line between convenience and compromise is increasingly blurred.

Instructors who embody this integrated approach do not simply teach about faith; they teach from it. They model hospitality, patience, and wisdom in how they structure their courses, how they engage students, and how they evaluate learning. They are not intimidated by new tools, nor are they enslaved to them. Instead, they help students develop the habits of heart and mind necessary to live faithfully in a digital age.

This includes cultivating humility in the face of complexity, curiosity in the face of change, and hope in the face of uncertainty.

Ultimately, tech-savvy yet soul-rich pedagogy is not about keeping up with trends or resisting change. It is about bearing witness—witness to a way of learning, leading, and living that is grounded in Christ, guided by the Spirit, and accountable to the community of faith. It trains students not just to navigate the tools of their age, but to serve the people of their time with integrity, compassion, and spiritual depth.

## Conclusion

The soul is not shaped by efficiency, nor is wisdom formed in haste. As artificial intelligence becomes increasingly present in theological education, seminaries must remember that formation is not a technical outcome but a spiritual one. While AI can assist with content delivery, cognitive development, and logistical support, it cannot cultivate love for God, reverence for mystery, or compassion for others. Those qualities are born through mentorship, practiced in spiritual disciplines, and nurtured in community.

The future of theological education must be both technologically conversant and spiritually grounded. Neglecting either side risks the integrity of the task. But when educators hold both together, teaching students to use new tools without losing their souls, they prepare leaders who can minister with wisdom, depth, and joy in a world that desperately needs all three. In such a vision, AI becomes not a threat, but a servant—a tool that, when rightly ordered, supports the formation of Christ-like leaders for the Church and the world.

# Chapter 13
## The Future of Theological Teaching in an AI World

### Introduction

The rise of artificial intelligence is not simply a technological shift—it is a cultural, moral, and educational transformation. For seminaries and theological institutions, this transformation offers both promise and peril. AI reshapes how we access information, engage with ideas, and interact with each other. It influences how students learn, how educators teach, and how communities of faith understand knowledge and wisdom. The future of theological teaching will not be immune to these shifts, and it should not be. But it must be prepared to engage them theologically, critically, and faithfully. This chapter explores how emerging technologies will influence the future of theological education and proposes a way forward that holds fast to our deepest commitments while embracing the possibilities of an AI-infused world.

### Emerging Technologies and Theological Education

Emerging technologies are reshaping the educational landscape with astonishing speed, and theological institutions are increasingly encountering both the challenges and opportunities they bring. From artificial intelligence and machine learning to virtual reality, natural language processing, and adaptive learning systems, these tools are no longer futuristic novelties—they are rapidly integrated into the practices of teaching, research, and ministry preparation. Theological educators must ask not only how these technologies work, but what kind of formation they promote, and what kind of theological imagination they require.

AI, for instance, is capable of parsing massive volumes of data, synthesizing research, offering linguistic translation, and even mimicking pastoral responses in chat-based simulations. Virtual and augmented reality are beginning to offer immersive experiences of biblical geography, historical reenactments, or liturgical worship across centuries and cultures. These tools can extend the reach of the classroom, offering access to rich theological learning for students in rural, under-resourced, or international settings. AI-powered tools can generate contextualized study guides, simulate ministry challenges for practicum learning, and facilitate collaborative writing, enabling more inclusive and interdisciplinary engagement.

Moreover, these technologies hold the promise of accessibility. Students with learning differences, language barriers, or geographic limitations may find greater ease participating in theological education when content is dynamically adapted or mediated through assistive technologies. Digitally enriched classrooms can include voices and traditions from across the globe, enabling a truly catholic engagement with the Church's wisdom. Courses that once required physical presence can now be redesigned as dynamic hybrid spaces — where real-time interaction is complemented by asynchronous reflection and AI-powered feedback loops.

Yet the benefits of these technologies must be weighed with care. They are not neutral tools; they carry embedded assumptions about learning, authority, and knowledge. For example, algorithms may prioritize efficiency over depth, personalization over communal formation, or novelty over tradition. Without theological framing, the tools may subtly reshape what theological education values—replacing wonder with convenience, or wisdom with information retrieval. The risk is not just technological dependency, but the distortion of education itself into a data-driven exercise rather than a formative journey toward discernment and spiritual maturity.

This is why theological educators must approach emerging technologies not merely as adopters, but as interpreters. They must become fluent in the language of innovation while remaining grounded in Scripture, tradition, and the lived practices of the Church. Rather than asking how to keep up with the latest tools, the question must become: How do these tools help or hinder the work of forming faithful, wise, and compassionate leaders for the Church and the world? This posture requires curiosity, caution, and above all, a vision of theological education that is deep enough to withstand the cultural currents of digital acceleration.

If emerging technologies are to serve theological education well, they must be baptized into a richer telos—a purpose centered on love of God and neighbor, not technological novelty or academic prestige. This means developing frameworks for discernment, ethical guidelines for use, and pedagogical models that place formation above functionality. When shaped by theological imagination, emerging technologies can become instruments of hospitality, access, creativity, and depth—serving not as masters of the classroom, but as companions on the journey of faith and learning.

## Continuous Formation of Faculty and Students

In an era marked by constant technological advancement and cultural flux, the work of theological formation can no longer be confined to the traditional arc of seminary education. Faculty and students alike must embrace an ethos of continuous formation—a lifelong openness to learning, unlearning, adapting, and growing. As artificial intelligence and digital technologies evolve rapidly, the Seminary cannot remain a static institution; it must become a learning community in motion, characterized by humility, curiosity, and discernment.

For faculty, this means far more than acquiring technical skills or mastering the newest educational software. It calls for a deeper transformation of pedagogical imagination. Theological educators must reexamine their assumptions about authority, content delivery, and the nature of wisdom itself. They must explore how to incorporate AI into their teaching in ways that are theologically sound and pedagogically effective. This may involve experimenting with new tools in the classroom, but it also requires cultivating spiritual and intellectual resilience. As students arrive increasingly fluent in digital platforms and generative tools, educators must be prepared to mentor them not just in content, but in the ethics and habits of theological inquiry in a digital world.

Ongoing faculty development becomes essential—not just as professional enrichment, but as an act of vocational stewardship. Workshops, interdisciplinary dialogue, peer collaboration, and spiritual retreat must be part of the ecosystem of a healthy institution. Faculty must be supported in the complex task of teaching in ways that both engage emerging technologies and remain deeply rooted in the Christian tradition. This includes spaces for theological reflection on technological change, for wrestling with questions of authorship and formation, and for renewing their own sense of calling as shepherds of learning.

For students, continuous formation means cultivating the capacity to live faithfully and thoughtfully in a culture shaped by rapid innovation. They must not only learn to use AI, but to interpret it — to evaluate its promises, interrogate its assumptions, and resist its excesses. They must learn to ask better questions, to reflect theologically on the tools they use, and to see their learning not as a short-term transaction but as a lifelong pilgrimage. This means developing habits of attentiveness, self-examination, and integration across disciplines.

Spiritual disciplines play a vital role here, anchoring students in rhythms of prayer, study, and communal life that resist the shallowness of information culture. Mentorship and community discernment are equally essential, offering the kind of formative encounters that no algorithm can replicate. Students need mentors who will not only guide their thinking but also model lives of integrity, humility, and theological imagination.

Seminaries that embrace continuous formation — at every level — will be better equipped to prepare students for a lifetime of leadership in a changing world. They will recognize that formation is not a finished product upon graduation, but a process that unfolds over decades of ministry, struggle, learning, and listening. In such communities, AI becomes a tool for ongoing growth, not a shortcut to immediate results. The institution becomes less a place of static content delivery and more a dynamic community of faithful learning, shaped by the Spirit and attentive to the world.

## Building Communities of Discernment and Innovation

The future of theological teaching in an AI world will not be shaped by technological tools alone but by the communities that use them — and how they choose to use them. As seminaries and theological institutions navigate this evolving terrain, they must prioritize the creation of communities marked by both discernment and innovation. These are not opposing values, but complementary virtues necessary for faithful engagement in a rapidly transforming world. Discernment ensures that theological education remains grounded in the wisdom of the Christian tradition, while innovation keeps it responsive to new challenges and opportunities. Together, they form the foundation for a pedagogy that is both timeless and timely.

Discernment begins with the acknowledgment that not every technological advancement is inherently good or appropriate for formation. Communities of discernment are willing to ask hard questions about what tools are used, why they are used, and what they produce in students. These questions go beyond functionality to matters of theology, ethics, and spiritual health. For instance, does the use of AI in sermon preparation cultivate dependence on external tools, or does it enhance the student's own exegetical and homiletical imagination? Does automated feedback deepen learning, or flatten the nuance of pastoral discernment? In discerning these tensions, the community must draw on Scripture, ecclesial tradition, communal wisdom, and prayer.

This discernment, however, must not result in stagnation. A theological institution that merely resists change becomes brittle and disconnected from the world it seeks to serve. Innovation is required — not for novelty's sake, but to respond to real needs with creativity and faith. Communities of innovation cultivate an openness to experimentation: testing new models of hybrid learning, incorporating AI-driven tools with accountability, and designing courses that integrate theological depth with technological fluency. Such innovation must be missional, not market-driven—focused on equipping students for the realities of contemporary ministry rather than chasing academic trends or consumer appeal.

To build such communities, institutional culture matters. Faculty, administrators, students, and staff must be invited into shared reflection on technology and pedagogy. This includes formal structures such as faculty workshops and curriculum reviews, but also informal spaces for conversation, feedback, and collaborative inquiry. Policies surrounding AI use must emerge not from top-down enforcement, but from shared theological commitments and ethical consensus. In this way, seminaries model for students how to make wise, community-rooted decisions about technology in their own future ministries.

These communities are also spiritual communities. They gather not just to analyze trends, but to worship, to pray, to listen to the voice of the Spirit amid the noise of digital acceleration. They recognize that innovation without spiritual grounding leads to disintegration, and that discernment without courageous action leads to fear-based inertia. Rooted in Christ and animated by the Spirit, they become spaces where theological imagination is nurtured, and where the future is welcomed not with anxiety, but with hope.

In such communities, students are not simply taught about theology—they are formed as theologians. They learn how to navigate a world of AI not as passive consumers or anxious resisters, but as wise leaders and discerning shepherds. And they graduate not only with tools in hand, but with hearts attuned to the deeper call of God amid a changing world.

## Conclusion

The future of theological teaching in an AI world will not be determined by machines, but by the choices we make as educators, students, and communities of faith. Technology will continue to evolve, and with it, the possibilities for learning, connection, and formation. But the core questions remain the same: Who are we becoming? What kind of leaders are we forming? How can we remain faithful to the gospel in a world shaped by algorithms and automation?

The seminaries that flourish in this future will be those that hold fast to their theological convictions while engaging the digital age with courage and creativity. They will resist both nostalgia and novelty, instead embodying a pedagogy rooted in Christ, attentive to the Spirit, and responsive to the needs of the Church and the world. In such communities, AI will not replace theological teaching—it will serve it. And theological education will continue to be a place where wisdom is pursued, souls are formed, and the next generation of leaders is prepared to serve with clarity, compassion, and conviction.

# Conclusion
## Forming Faithful Leaders for an AI-Integrated Church

Theological education is entering a new epoch — one shaped not only by ecclesial and cultural change, but by the rise of artificial intelligence and its rapid influence on how we think, learn, communicate, and minister. What was once a novelty is now a daily presence: AI tools that assist with writing, translation, research, feedback, and even pastoral simulation have begun reshaping the seminary classroom. For educators committed to forming wise and faithful Christian leaders, this shift presents both opportunity and danger.

Throughout this book, we have explored the potential of AI to assist theological instruction across the full spectrum of Bloom's Taxonomy — helping students remember key terms, understand doctrines, apply theology in pastoral contexts, analyze complex texts, evaluate theological claims, and create new expressions of Christian witness. We have also reflected on how AI might be used in capstone projects, spiritual formation, hybrid classrooms, and even theological case studies — always with the goal of serving the deeper vocation of formation, not replacing it.

But alongside possibility comes risk. We have named the dangers of plagiarism, epistemic laziness, theological shallowness, and disconnection from community. We have considered how over-reliance on machine intelligence can compromise the soul-shaping work of theological education — work that demands slowness, relationship, struggle, and prayer. We have argued that while AI may be a powerful tool, it must never be treated as a theological authority or a surrogate for human discernment.

What then is the calling of the theological educator in this emerging world?

First, to resist fear and embrace wisdom. New technologies need not be rejected out of hand, nor embraced uncritically. Discernment—not novelty or nostalgia—must guide our use of AI in seminary settings. This means cultivating communities of reflection, inviting students into conversations about authorship, truth, and formation, and crafting learning environments where human insight is elevated, not outsourced.

It is also to recover a robust theological imagination. Teaching in the age of AI requires more than technical skill; it requires a renewed vision of what it means to teach theologically. The classroom is not just a place for information delivery, but a space of encounter—where students meet not only new ideas but the living God. AI can assist in this work, but only when guided by educators who model humility, curiosity, and love for both their students and the Church.

And finally, it is to remember the heart of our vocation: to form people who can think theologically, lead pastorally, and live faithfully. AI will continue to grow in capability, but it cannot pray. It cannot love a congregation. It cannot wrestle with Scripture in the night watches or discern the Spirit's whisper in the chaos of ministry. That is the work of people shaped by grace, grounded in tradition, and called by God.

As we look to the future, may we teach not only with excellence, but with reverence. May we steward new technologies without surrendering our deepest values. And may we send forth graduates who are not merely competent in a digital world, but courageous and Christ-shaped—ready to serve a Church that is being renewed by the Spirit in every generation, including this one.

# Appendix A
# Bloom's Taxonomy Checklist for Theological Courses

This checklist is designed to help faculty ensure that theological courses engage students across all levels of Bloom's Taxonomy, from foundational knowledge to creative theological expression.

## Remembering
☐ Are students asked to recall key theological terms, dates, Scriptures, or concepts?

☐ Do assessments include opportunities for memorization and review?

☐ Have you provided resources (e.g., flashcards, timelines, AI-generated quizzes) to support recall?

## Understanding
☐ Do students explain theological concepts in their own words?

☐ Are they interpreting Scripture, tradition, or doctrine meaningfully?

☐ Are concept maps or AI summaries used to clarify ideas?

## Applying
☐ Are students invited to apply theology to real-world ministry scenarios?

☐ Have you included simulations, case studies, or role-playing (AI-enhanced or otherwise)?

☐ Do assignments bridge doctrine and practice?

## Analyzing

☐ Are students comparing theological viewpoints or scriptural interpretations?

☐ Do they identify assumptions, logical structures, and relationships?

☐ Are tools available for mapping arguments or contrasting theological systems?

## Evaluating

☐ Do students make informed theological or ethical judgments?

☐ Are they evaluating arguments, sermons, or traditions critically?

☐ Have you scaffolded space for reasoned debate and reflection?

## Creating

☐ Are students producing original work—sermons, reflections, liturgies, or theological frameworks?

☐ Do assignments encourage synthesis of learning across disciplines?

☐ Is there a capstone or final project that invites innovation?

# Appendix B
# Annotated List of AI Tools for Seminary Educators

This annotated list outlines a variety of AI tools that can support teaching, learning, and administration in theological education.

## ChatGPT / Claude / Gemini
Use for drafting, idea generation, language modeling, and theological dialogue. Great for student tutoring, prompt generation, or sermon drafting (with caution).

## Quizlet / Brainscape (AI-enhanced)
Create or generate flashcards for biblical languages, theological terms, or historical figures. Helpful for review and exam preparation.

## Perplexity.ai
A research assistant that provides source-backed responses and encourages deeper inquiry. Best used for comparative theological exploration or guided research.

## Scite / Elicit
AI research tools that locate and summarize academic sources. Useful for students to write papers or evaluate scholarly perspectives.

**Curipod / Canva Magic / Genially**

Presentation and lesson planning tools with generative AI features. Supports lecture prep and visual learning resources.

**Diffit / MagicSchool.ai**

Tools for adapting content across levels of difficulty or generating classroom materials. Effective for differentiated instruction in mixed-preparation classrooms.

**Otter.ai / Fireflies**

AI transcription and summarization tools useful for recording and reviewing class discussions or faculty meetings.

**Semantic Scholar / ResearchRabbit**

AI-assisted scholarly databases for theological and biblical studies research. Encourages students to trace conversations across disciplines.

# Appendix C
## Sample Course Syllabi with AI Integration

Below is a condensed example of how AI might be integrated into a theological course syllabus.

**Course Title:** Introduction to Systematic Theology
**Instructor:** Dr. Jane Doe

**Learning Outcomes:**
- Understand and articulate key doctrines of the Christian faith.
- Analyze theological arguments using classical and contemporary sources.
- Apply theological insights to ministry contexts.

**AI-Integrated Activities:**
*Week 2:* Use ChatGPT to summarize the Nicene Creed and compare interpretations across denominations.
*Week 4:* Submit an AI-generated outline of a theological argument (students must annotate and critique).
*Week 6:* Role-play a doctrinal debate using an AI-generated character profile (e.g., Anselm or Barth).
*Week 9:* Use semantic search tools to find and evaluate two scholarly sources on atonement theories.
*Final Project:* Students may use AI to generate a sermon outline or doctrinal comparison—but must document all AI use and reflect on theological integrity.

**Policy Note:** Students must disclose all use of AI tools in written assignments and adhere to academic integrity guidelines.

# Appendix D
# AI Prompt Bank for Theological Contexts

These sample prompts can be used by educators or students for productive theological interaction with AI tools.

### For Biblical Studies
"Summarize the themes of the Gospel of John in paragraph form."
"Compare the covenantal theology in Genesis 12 and Galatians 3."

### For Systematic Theology
"Generate a list of key theological terms used in Trinitarian theology and define them."
"Compare Calvin's and Wesley's views of sanctification in outline format."

### For Church History
"Create a dialogue between Martin Luther and John Henry Newman on authority and tradition."
"Summarize the theological outcomes of the Council of Chalcedon."

### For Practical Theology
"Simulate a pastoral counseling session with a congregant experiencing burnout."
"Draft a reflection on ministry ethics in an urban context with generative AI critique."

## For Spiritual Formation

"Write a guided prayer based on Psalm 51, suitable for a seminary chapel service."

"Offer a spiritual practice of attentiveness rooted in Ignatian tradition."

# Appendix E
## Faculty Development Plan for Implementing AI

This sample plan offers a structure for helping seminary faculty engage with AI ethically and effectively.

### Phase 1: Orientation and Theological Framing
- Host a faculty colloquium on "The Ethics and Promise of AI in Christian Pedagogy."
- Assign readings that address theology of technology, human agency, and discernment.

### Phase 2: Skill-Building and Experimentation
- Offer workshops on using AI tools (ChatGPT, Otter.ai, Elicit) for research and teaching.
- Encourage faculty to revise one syllabus to integrate AI-supported activities.

### Phase 3: Piloting and Peer Feedback
- Create faculty learning communities for sharing syllabi and classroom experiences.
- Pilot AI-integrated modules in a few courses; gather student feedback and reflect together.

### Phase 4: Institutionalization and Policy Development
- Develop a Seminary-wide AI usage policy with input from faculty, students, and administrators.
- Include AI ethics training in new faculty orientation and ongoing pedagogy seminars.

## Phase 5: Reflection and Revision

- Regularly revisit AI use through theological and pedagogical lenses.
- Support sabbaticals, writing projects, or conference presentations on theological education and AI.